Intermediate

D0197715

Just Right

Jeremy Harmer

Grammar materials co-author: Hester Lott

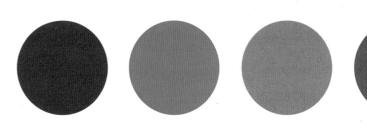

Student's Book

Marshall Cavendish
Education

EFL Zone   Includes mini grammar book.

Text acknowledgements

pp 6, 80, 102, 124, 135, bottom left 143, Macmillan English Dictionary for Advanced Learners by Michael Rundell and Gwyneth Fox, ©Bloomsbury Publishing 2002. Reprinted by permission of Macmillan, Oxford; p18, Cambridge Learners Dictionary, ©Cambridge University Press; pp 26, 37, 49, 57, 68, 89, 111, top left & right 143, Longman Dictionary of Contemporary English New Edition, ©Pearson Education Limited, 1978, 2003; p28, based on Shopping by John Crace, ©Guardian; p38, Backpackerland, based on an article by Jason Burke, Observer Newspapers; p46, No Home, No Job, No Worries, ©CJ Stone, from The Big Issue 11-17 August 1997; p71, How to make those New Year's resolutions stick, ©Dr Pauline Wallin; p85, Neighbour bites dog in fence dispute, ©Jeremy Harmer, reprinted by permission of Pearson Education Limited; p99 Wired? Not Worth it! based on Dumbing Us Down ©Theodore Roznak, News Internationalist issue 26, December 1996; p146, Rachel, taken from Trumpet Voluntary, ©Jeremy Harmer.

© 2004 Marshall Cavendish Ltd

First published 2004 by Marshall Cavendish Ltd

Reprinted 2005 and 2007

ISBN 978-0-462-00719-9

Marshall Cavendish is a member of the Times Publishing Group

Marshall Cavendish Education
119 Wardour Street
London W1F 0UW

Designed by Hart McLeod, Cambridge
Editorial development by Ocelot Publishing, Oxford
Illustrations by Yane Christiansen, Rod Hunt, Jennifer Ward, Phil Healey and Francis Fung

Printed and bound by Times Offset (M) Sdn. Bhd. Malaysia

Photo acknowledgements

p6 top left to right: ©Russ Widstrand/alamy.com; ©Pictor International/ImageState/alamy.com; ©Jon Mitchell/Lightroom Photos/alamy.com; ©Burke/Tiolo/Brand X Pictures/alamy.com; ©SW Productions/Brand X Pictures/alamy.com; bottom left to right: ©Tom Tracy Photography/alamy.com; ©Tom Tracy Photography/Stock Connection, Inc/alamy.com; ©Novastock/Stock Connection. Inc/alamy.com; ©Goodshoot/alamy.com; ©image100/alamy.com; p11 ©Robert Llewellyn/ImageState/alamy.com; p12 ©Reeve Photography; p15 tl, ©Peter Turnley/Corbis, tc, ©Robert Harding World Imagery/Robert Harding Picture Library Ltd/alamy.com; bc, England/Art Explosion; tr, © Corbis; p16 ©Zefa/Studio Wartenberg; p19 ©Robert Llewellyn/Image State/alamy.com; p21 ©Rex Features; p24 ©Stock Connection, Inc/alamy.com; p26 left to right: ©Chris Knapton/alamy.com, ©Sally & Richard Greenhill/alamy.com, ©Worldwide Picture Library/alamy.com, ©Pictor International/ImageState/alamy.com; p31 left to right: ©Mark Sykes/alamy.com, ©Mark Lewis/alamy.com, ©Image 100/alamy.com, ©Abode/alamy.com; p33 top: ©Topham Picturepoint; bottom: ©Pictor International/ImageState/alamy.com; p36 top: ©Corbis; left to right: ©Pictures Colour Library, ©Sami Sarkis/alamy.com; ©Mark Anderson/RubberBall/alamy.com; ©Jackson Smith/alamy.com; bottom left to right: ©Mark Anderson/alamy.com; Jackson Smith/alamy.com; ©Ken Hawkins/Focus Group, LLC/alamy.com; ©Image Source Ltd/alamy.com; John Foxx/alamy.com; p38 Pictures Colour Library; p42 both: Robert Harding/World Imagery/Robert Harding Picture Library Ltd/alamy.com; p46 Tim Heatherington/Network Photographers; p49 ©Paul McMullim/alamy.com; ©Spectrum Colour Library; ©Peter Brooker/Rex Features; ©Topham Picturepoint; p51 ©Image100/alamy.com; p53 ©Ariel Skelley/Corbis; p58 tl, ©Bettman/Corbis, tr, ©Rex Features, bl, ©Corbis; p60 both: ©Corbis; p62 ©Reeve Photography; p63 Portrait of John Evelyn (1620-1706) by English School (17th Century), Roy Miles Fine Paintings/Bridgeman Art Library; tr, The Artist's Daughter c.1927-28 (oil on canvas by Augustus Edwin John (1878-1961)) National Gallery of Victoria, Melbourne, Australia/Bridgman Art Library Felton bequest; Mr and Mrs Andrews c.1748-9 (oil on canvas) (detail of 467) by Thomas Gainsborough (1727-88) National Gallery London UK/Bridgeman Art Library; p73 a & c ©Corbis; b ©Rex Features; d ©Doug Scott/Powerstock; p88 all: ©Reeve Photography; p98 a ©Braun Oral B, c & q ©Art Explosion Royalty Free, b, f, i ©Sony UK, e ©Sharp Electronics, all others Topham Picturepoint; p101 ©Corbis; p105 ©Reeve Photography; p110 (1) Summer of the Seventeenth Doll, by Ray Lawler, first published by Currency Press, Sidney Australia in 1978, (2) Hodder and Stoughton; (3) ©Topham Picturepoint; (4) ©Ronald Grant Archive; p112 top: ©Paul Almasy/Corbis, middle and bottom: ©Ronald Grant Archive; p116 By permission of Harper Collins Publishers, by permission of Penguin Books, by permission of Random House, by permission of Faber and Faber for their book cover 'Kitchen', by Banana Yoshimoto; p119 a ©Rex Features, b & c ©Corbis, d ©ImagesState/Alamy, e ©Karl Weatherly/Corbis, f ©Eddy Lemaistre/Photo & Co/Corbis; p123 ©Popperfoto/alamy.com; p124 ©Popperfoto; p126 ©Reeve Photography; p130 ©Redferns, p131 top to bottom: ©Erik Penozich/Rex Features, ©Jon Feingersh/Corbis; ©Rex Features; p133 b, e, g, h & i, ©Topham Picturepoint, a ©Dimitri Lundt/Corbis, c ©Mitchell Gerber/Corbis, d, f, k ©Royalty Free/Corbis, j ©Tom Stewart/Corbis; p135 left to right: ©Dave Jimenez, ©Peter Bowater/alamy.com, ©Art Explosion/Recreation; p143 clockwise from the top right, ©Mark Andersen/RubberBall/alamy.com; ©Yang Liu/Corbis; ©J Stock/Stockshot/alamy.com; ©Wally McNamee/Corbis; ©BananaStock/alamy.com; ©Art-Line Productions/Brand X Pictures/alamy.com; ©Image Source/alamy.com; ©Fog City Productions/Brand X Pictures/alamy.com; ©Mark Andersen/RubberBall/alamy.com; ©RubberBall Productions/RubberBall/alamy.com; centre left, Bill Bachmann/alamy.com; centre right, Alan Bailey/RubberBall/alamy.com; pp154 & 157 centre ©Rex Features, (1) ©RubberBall/alamy.com; (2, 9 & 10) ©image 100/alamy.com; (3) ©Corbis, (4) ©RubberBall/alamy.com; (5) ©Image Source/alamy.com; (6) ©Image Source/alamy.com; (7) ©Corbis; (8) ©ImageState/alamy.com; (11) ©Luca DiCecco/alamy.com; (12) ©Topham Picturepoint; p155 Marc Chagall: The Poet Reclining, 1915 ©ADAGP, Paris and DACS, London 2004, ©Paul Lowe/Panos Pictures; p158 Marc Chagall: The Green Donkey ©ADAGP, Paris and DACS, London 2004, ©Paul Lowe/Panos Pictures; p159 by kind permission of David Wilde ©2002 Delphian Records Ltd.

Contents

Skills

Language

UNIT 1
What are you like?

→ present simple
→ present continuous
→ personal qualities
→ meeting people

Speaking: comparing answers

1 **Discussion** Look at the pictures. Which job would you most like to do? Which job would you least like to do? Why? Compare your answers with a partner's.

design engineer

footballer

journalist

orchestral conductor

primary teacher

firefighter

soldier

nurse

personal assistant (PA)

refuse collector

2 Who should be paid more? Put the jobs in order where *1 = the highest salary* and *10 = the lowest salary*. Compare your answers with a partner's.

●●● Using a dictionary: definitions and examples

3 Look at the entries for *assertive* and *sensitive* and answer the questions.

asse..... /ə'sɜ:-/
claim that something is true
assertive /ə'sɜ:tɪv/ adj behaving in a confident way in which you are quick to express your opinions and feelings: *You need to be more assertive to succeed in business.* —**assertively** adv, **assertiveness** noun [U]
.... /'....-/ .... [T]

sensitive /'sensətɪv/ adj ★★★
3 showing that you care about someone or something and do not want to cause offence: *This is a difficult case which needs sensitive and skilful handling.* ♦ **+to** *The police should be more sensitive to the needs of local communities.*

a Which are the definitions?
b Which are the examples?

Vocabulary: character description

4 **Language research** Look at the list of adjectives. Tick the ones you know. Look up the ones you don't know.

▶ assertive	▶ enthusiastic	▶ intelligent	▶ pleasant
▶ confident	▶ friendly	▶ interesting	▶ romantic
▶ considerate	▶ happy	▶ kind	▶ sensitive
▶ decisive	▶ honest	▶ loyal	▶ sincere
▶ emotional	▶ hospitable	▶ patient	▶ sympathetic

5 Work in pairs. Choose any three of the professions in Activity 1 on page 6. Using the words from Activity 4, describe the ideal character for them.

Example: *The ideal nurse is friendly, patient and sympathetic.*

Find other pairs who chose the same professions and see if you agree.

6 We can give words opposite meanings by adding a prefix like *un-*, *in-*, *im-*, *dis-*, etc.

Example: *necessary – unnecessary*
appear – disappear

Give the opposite meaning for each word in Activity 4 by choosing the correct prefix. The first three are done for you.

un-	*in-*	*im-*	*dis-*
unassertive *unconfident*	*inconsiderate*		

7 Look again at the professions in Activity 1. Using the words you made in Activity 6, describe people who are bad at their occupations.

Example: *An unfriendly, impatient and unsympathetic nurse is not very good at her job!*

Reading: questionnaire

8 Read the following personality questionnaire and choose an answer
for each question. Compare your answers with a partner's.

What are you like?

1 At the end of a romantic film when the girl and the boy finally say they love each other, do you:
  a wish you'd gone to a film with lots of guns and explosions?
  b feel bored?
  c cry?

2 You watch a friend or a relative win in a sports competition. Do you:
  a clap politely but happily?
  b clap enthusiastically, and encourage other people to do the same?
  c jump up and down, cheering as loudly as you can?

3 It's Friday evening. You've had a long and tiring week. Do you:
  a stay at home and read a book?
  b go to a show or a film with a friend?
  c go to a club with a group of friends?

4 Someone wants to talk to you about their problems while you are watching a TV programme. Do you:
  a say 'Not now, I'm watching television'?
  b continue to watch television while they talk?
  c turn off the television and listen attentively?

5 Your brother's friend rings to say that he's just arrived in your town, but you already have plans to go out with another friend. Do you:
  a say 'How lovely to hear from you. What a pity I'm just going out'?
  b try and find out how long he's going to stay before asking him over?
  c invite him to your house straightaway?

6 A friend criticises something new you are wearing. Do you:
  a say 'I don't care what you think. I like it'?
  b decide never to wear it again?
  c go home and change immediately?

7 Someone asks you to give them a lift in your car, but they want to go somewhere different from you. Do you:
  a say 'I'm sorry, I don't want to go that way'?
  b say 'Yes, but I wasn't going to go that way'?
  c say 'Yes of course', even though it's inconvenient?

8 At work your boss asks you if you can work at the weekend to finish an urgent job. Do you:
  a refuse politely and say 'The weekend is for my family'?
  b say 'I'm not sure. I need to think about it'?
  c agree immediately because you want to be helpful?

9 You don't feel like going to work or school because you went to a party last night. Do you:
  a call and say 'My friend isn't feeling very well. I'm staying at home to look after him'?
  b call and say you are ill?
  c go into work or school and try your best?

10 Someone falls off their bicycle in the street in front of you. Do you:
  a call out 'Are you OK?' but keep on walking?
  b run to get help?
  c keep walking because you have an important appointment and you don't want to be late?

9 **Discussion** What kind of person chooses a, b or c each time?

  Check your conclusions with the questionnaire key in Activity Bank 1 on page 151.

10 Find words in the questionnaire with the following meanings. The first letter of each word is given.

  a Someone who is linked to you by marriage or blood is a r*elative* .
  b If you do something with a lot of energy and passion you do it e................................. .
  c If you listen, read or watch very carefully, you do it a................................. .
  d If you say something bad about someone or something you c................................. them or it.
  e Something that is not helpful because it wastes your time is i................................. .
  f If you do something to the best of your ability you t................. y................. b................. .

11 Look at the questionnaire again and, in groups, write three more questions to investigate personality characteristics. Interview other members of the class using your questions.

Grammar: present tenses

12 Noticing language Look for present tense verbs in the questionnaire in Activity 8. Write down some of the examples of the present tenses you found and say what each one means.

13 Choose the correct form (present simple, e.g. *he runs,* or present continuous, e.g. *he is running*) of the verb in brackets.

Marek (**a** live) .... in London. He (**b** get up) .... at about six o'clock every morning and (**c** drive) .... to work. He (**d** work) .... in a big room because he needs lots of space. At work he (**e** wear) .... overalls, goggles and big gloves. At the moment he (**f** work) .... on a new sculpture for a main square in the city. He (**g** make) .... his sculpture from wood.

When he (**h** leave) .... work in the evening he (**i** drive) .... back home. He has dinner with his family and then he (**j** read) .... to his children before they go to sleep. At the moment they (**k** read) .... a book about a wizard called Harry Potter. When the children are asleep he (**l** watch) .... television with his wife. When he (**m** go) .... to sleep he (**n** dream) .... of wood and metal – and all the sculptures he is going to make one day.

If you have problems with this activity, look at **1A–1C in the Mini-grammar** in the booklet at the back.

14 Work in pairs. Talk about the people in the pictures. Use your imagination.

Ask questions with *when, what, how often,* etc.

Example: STUDENT A: What does Paul do in his act?
STUDENT B: He probably falls over, tries to ride a bicycle, that kind of thing.

Normally

Sally Jones, trapeze artist   Paul Jones, clown

Sally's and Paul's holiday pictures

Ask questions about the pictures.

Example: STUDENT A: What's Sally doing in the first picture?
STUDENT B: She's lying in the sun, reading a magazine and drinking a cola.

15 Choose the correct tense in the following sentences. Look at 1B–1D in the **Mini-grammar** for help.

a We are knowing / We know that you did it!

b Oh, this is dramatic! Peters is running / runs up to the wicket, is bowling / bowls the ball – and it is going / goes right through the batsman's legs.

c Hello. What? … I'm on the train … we just leave / are just leaving.

d Oh, stop it! You're always telling / You always tell me to tidy my room and it's not fair!

e There's no doubt about it. The weather gets / is getting warmer all the time. Global warming is a reality.

f When Oscar leaves / is leaving Sidney he is giving / gives a note to Lucinda. He tells / is telling her not to open it unless he doesn't return / isn't returning.

g Mary never wakes / is waking up on time and so she often misses / is missing the bus.

h … so your flight is leaving / leaves at 3.45 and you land / are landing in Kuala Lumpur at 5.00 am. The minibus is taking / takes you to the hotel …

i I'm working / work here until 8.00 tonight, then I meet / I'm meeting the band at the reception.

16 Use the present simple or the present continuous to complete the following tasks.

a Tell your neighbour about something ordinary that happened to you yesterday – as if it was a dramatic story or the plot of a film.

b Ask your neighbour to describe three people they know about – from life, films or books – who have particular habits (things they are always doing).

c Find out from your partner three things they think about circuses, three things they know for sure about a sport, three people they like, and three things they don't understand about geography and the physical world.

Functional language: meeting people

17 Before you listen to Track 1, read the dialogue and complete it with the following lines.

> Not much really.
>
> Oh, all right.
>
> Oh, I mean I only started last week. It's my first job. What about you?
>
> That sounds interesting.
>
> Yeah, nice to meet you too.

JANE: Come on, Polly, there's someone I'd like you to meet.

POLLY: (**a**) ....

JANE: Andy, this is Polly. She's in advertising too.

ANDY: Oh, hi. Nice to meet you.

POLLY: (**b**) ....

ANDY: What do you do in advertising?

POLLY: (**c**) ....

ANDY: Sorry?

POLLY: (**d**) ....

ANDY: Me? Oh well, I'm working on a TV commercial for an Internet bank at the moment.

POLLY: (**e**) ....

ANDY: Yes, yes it is.

Now listen to Track 1. Were you right?

18 In each box, match the words in the two columns to make statements or questions.

a There's someone	in advertising.
b Andy, this	I'd like you to meet.
c I'd like you	meet you.
d Polly's	is Polly.
e Nice to	to meet Andy.

f Are you	you do?
g Do you like	at the moment?
h How do you	know our host?
i What are you working on	what you do?
j What do	a friend of Polly's?

k Oh	coincidence! I'm an actor too.
l That	really?
m What a	sounds interesting.

Example: a *There's someone I'd like you to meet.*

19 Practice In groups of three, introduce each other as if you were meeting for the first time. Ask about the person's occupation. Use language from Activity 18.

Example: STUDENT A: *John, there's someone I'd like you to meet. ... This is Mary.*

STUDENT B: *Hello, Mary. What do you do?*

STUDENT C: *I'm a student.*

20 Role-play You are going to a party.

a Choose a name for yourself.

b Decide:

... what your occupation is.

... what you do in that occupation.

... whether or not you like it, and why.

... what you are working on / studying at the moment.

c Copy the table in Activity Bank 2 on page 151 and fill in your details.

d Now go to the party and talk to at least three people. Complete the table with their details as you talk.

Pronunciation: hearing sounds

21 **Say these words:**

small always organised four sort more

What sound do all the words share, /æ/ like *cat*, /ɔː/ like *call*, or /ʌ/ like *bus*?

22 **List which of the following words share the same sound as the words above.**

all arm door seem smell stare ought walk work store out saw

Now listen to Track 2 on the tape. Were you correct?

Listening: working in a man's world

23 **Listen to Track 3. This is an extract from an interview with April Considine. Can you guess which of the following is her occupation?**

- teacher
- design engineer
- doctor
- pilot

Look at Activity Bank 3 on page 151 to see if you were right.

24 **Listen to Track 4 and answer the following questions.**

a Who first encouraged April to be interested in engineering?

b On the whole, does April think that being a woman in a male environment is a good thing or a bad thing?

25 **Are the following sentences *True* or *False*? Write T or F in the brackets.**

a April's father is Irish. [ ]

b A glider is an aeroplane without an engine. [ ]

c April can fly a glider. [ ]

d April sometimes works at Marshall's at the weekend. [ ]

e April's work is usually checked by four other people. [ ]

f A hangar is a big building where you put aeroplanes. [ ]

g April works in the hangars. [ ]

h There were many girls in the hangars. [ ]

i Nobody spoke to April in the hangars. [ ]

26 **Check the meaning of the following phrases. Listen to Track 4 again and tick (✓) the things that April says are important in her job. Put a cross (✗) beside the things that she does not mention.**

It is important to:

a ... arrive and leave work on time. [ ]

b ... be a hard worker. [ ]

c ... be able to communicate. [ ]

d ... be able to prove yourself. [ ]

e ... be able to work on your own. [ ]

f ... be decisive. [ ]

g ... be courteous. [ ]

h ... be energetic. [ ]

i ... be good-looking. [ ]

j ... be organised. [ ]

k ... be well-dressed. [ ]

l ... be young and enthusiastic. [ ]

m ... go out in the evening with colleagues. [ ]

n ... love your job. [ ]

o ... make sure it's right. [ ]

p ... show initiative. [ ]

27 April used the following expressions in Track 4. Explain the meaning of the words and phrases in blue.

a He's always been really keen on engineering.
b He's always working on cars and bits and pieces.
c He did a little bit himself.
d I got involved with that.
e It still comes down to you.
f ... if you sit there and just do the minimum.
g They all keep an eye on what I'm doing.
h ... to find out how I was getting on.

28 Ask your partner what they need to succeed in their occupation.

Example: STUDENT A: *What do you need to be a good student?*

STUDENT B: *Well, I suppose you've got to be conscientious, you've got to be able to work on your own – and it helps if you're a little bit intelligent!*

Writing: personal reports

29 After reading a teacher's reports on her students, the college head has asked the teacher to write them again – but to be completely positive this time. Which student is the teacher writing about in the second (positive) group of reports *a–c*?

Justin Harrison
In spite of his enthusiastic and friendly nature, Justin is often far too emotional. His romantic ideas often amuse the rest of the class and he gets very upset because of their behaviour. This is a pity because he is intelligent and often shows initiative.

Sally Greenspan
Despite her intelligence, Sally is extremely assertive and rather inconsiderate to other members of the class. She is often impatient with her classmates and unsympathetic to their difficulties.

John Armitage
Although John tries his best, he is just not very intelligent. He does not seem able to show initiative, and because he is not very decisive he is not making much progress.

a _____ *is a decisive and intelligent worker, shows considerable initiative and is very enthusiastic.*

b _____ *is conscientious, friendly and pleasant, and a pleasure to have in the class with us.*

c _____ *is a happy, sensitive student, obviously sincere, and a loyal classmate. Contributions to class discussion from this student are always interesting.*

30 Look at how the different linking words in the reports are followed by different grammatical patterns.

LINKING WORDS

- The words *although* and *because* are followed by a clause containing a subject and a verb:
  Although John tries his best ...
- *... because he is not very decisive ...*

- *In spite of*, *despite* and *because of* are followed by a noun or *-ing* form verb:
  In spite of his enthusiastic and friendly nature ...
- *Despite her intelligence ...*
- *... because of their behaviour ...*

31 Now combine phrases and sentences from Box A with phrases and sentences from Box C using one of the linking words in Box B.

A	B	C
He is happy	although	getting up early.
Stephen is very excited		he has just won the lottery.
He played a good game	in spite of	he is not very big.
She missed the train		she is not very intelligent.
Arran is a good football player	because	his lottery win.
Mark is not very popular		his hard work.
He failed his exam	despite	his friendly and enthusiastic manner.
Sadia passed her exam		feeling ill.
	because of	

32 Write two reports about Andrew Tregarron using the appropriate information given in the box below. In the first report you should be honest, and in the second more positive. Follow the patterns explained in Activity 30.

> a fast worker
>
> makes mistakes
>
> not very popular (tries too
> hard to make friends)
>
> obsessed with music
>
> sometimes careless
>
> tries his best to make friends
>
> very creative
>
> very musical

Review: grammar and functional language

33 Choose the correct form of the verb in brackets.

Kim is in her final year of a psychology degree at the University of East Anglia in England. Next week she has final exams so there are no classes. Like all the other students on her course this week she (**a** revise) .... instead.

But Kim (**b** not study) .... very hard right now. She (**c** sit) .... in the garden of her house, (**d** read) .... her notes. It is a beautiful day. Birds (**e** sing) .... in the trees. She (**f** sit/not usually) .... in the garden like this during term time. Normally she (**g** take) .... the bus to the university at nine o'clock and (**h** study) .... all day. She (**i** have) .... lunch at about one with her friends, especially Alice and Gemma. But today Alice (**j** visit) .... her grandmother and Gemma (**k** take) .... part in an athletics event. Still, her brother is home from his job as a junior doctor in Scotland. She can hear him now. He (**l** talk) .... to his girlfriend on the telephone.

The sun (**m** get) .... hotter. Maybe revising is not a good idea. Perhaps she could ring Alice and they could go for a swim.

34 Look at the pictures below. What personal qualities do people need to do these jobs?

  a Make sentences which describe their routine.

  b What are they (probably) doing now?

35 **Dialogue writing** Which two people, living or dead, would you most like to meet at a party? Write a dialogue in which you and your friend are introduced to them.

Example: SARA: *Hello, Mark. I'd like you to meet Ludwig Van Beethoven.*

  MARK: *Hello, Mr Beethoven. Nice to meet you.*

  BEETHOVEN: *Sorry?*

  MARK: *Nice to meet you.*

  BEETHOVEN: *I'm sorry, I can't hear you. I'm a little deaf.*

  MARK: *I said NICE TO MEET YOU!*

Review: vocabulary

Word List

assertive confident conscientious considerate decisive design engineer doctor emotional enthusiastic firefighter footballer friendly happy honest hospitable impatient intelligent interesting journalist kind loyal nurse occupation orchestral conductor organised patient personal assistant (PA) pilot pleasant primary teacher refuse collector romantic salary sensitive sincere soldier sympathetic

Word Plus

a little bit	to be keen on
bits and pieces	to be organised
it comes down to you	to do the minimum
on your own	to keep an eye on
to be able to	to make sure
to be involved with	to prove yourself
to be getting on	to show initiative

36 Which are your five favourite words from the Word List here?

37 Write words from the Word List for these two meaning groups.

  a occupations
  b characteristics

Pronunciation

38 a Complete the table with the three- and four-syllable words from the Word List. Where is the stress in each case?

three syllables	four syllables
asser*tive*	con*si*derate

Listen to Track 5 and check your answers.

  b How many different ways is the letter 'c' pronounced in the words in the Word List?

Listen to Track 6 and check your answer.

39 **The opposites game** Team A says a word from the Word List. Team B says the opposite using a prefix or another word.

Example: TEAM A: *assertive*

  TEAM B: *unassertive*

Score one point for each correct answer.

40 **Speaking** Work in pairs. Student A phones Student B to find out how they have been getting on in their job/studies. How many Word plus phrases (above) can you include in your conversation?

UNIT 2
A narrow escape

→ past simple → past continuous
→ past perfect → stronger adjectives
→ intensifying verbs
→ giving opinions

Listening: pirates

1 Look at the picture. Is the garden safe? What dangers might there be for a young child, if an adult wasn't watching?

2 Two people are talking about a dangerous situation in a garden.

a Listen to Track 7 and answer the following questions.

1 How old was the narrator?
2 What had the narrator's mother done? Why?
3 'I think I know what's coming.' Can you guess what's going to happen next?

b Listen to Track 8 and answer the following questions.

1 Why did the narrator get in the trunk?
2 What happened immediately after that and what did the narrator do?
3 'So what happened?' Can you guess?

c Listen to Track 9 and answer the following questions.

1 What did the narrator's mother suddenly realise?
2 What did she see?
3 What did she do and how did the narrator feel?

3 What do the following words, used in Tracks 8 and 9, mean?

a pirate
b trapped
c upstairs
d unconscious
e shocked
f claustrophobic

4 Listen to Tracks 7 to 9 again and complete the sentences below with the missing words.

a ... there was an incident once, well, it could have ended in tragedy. It was ....

b ... and almost immediately got the idea that one of the trunks could be a boat, a pirate ship, that kind of thing. I thought it ....

c What do you think? Of course I was. Pretty soon .... to be honest.

d It only took her a second to realise what had happened. She ....

e ... she pulled me out, half-unconscious, ... and frightened out of my wits!

● ● ● Pronunciation: spelling and sounds

5 Listen to Track 10 to hear the different pronunciations of the letter 'a'. Put the blue words into the correct columns.

I was running around playing.   Old-fashioned things.   So I came round the corner …
… and saw these trunks …   I was trapped.   … again and again.   So, what happened?
So she called my name, she said …

a /æ/ c*a*t, h*a*t	b /ɔ:/ f*ou*r, m*o*re	c /ə/ *a* bottle *of* milk	d /e/ m*a*ny, s*ai*d	e /eɪ/ p*ay*, tod*ay*
				playing

6 Can you add any more words to the columns? Can you find any other ways to pronounce the letter 'a'?

● ●

7 Have you ever had a narrow escape? Has anyone you know had one? Tell the class about it.

Vocabulary: stronger adjectives

8 We sometimes want to use stronger adjectives when describing things.

A: I was late for work again this morning.
B: Was your boss angry?
A: Angry? She was furious!

Match the following adjectives with the adjectives in the table.

big
dirty
fantastic
fascinating
freezing
funny
furious
hot
surprising
terrible
terrifying

Ordinary adjectives	Stronger adjectives
angry	*furious*
bad	
	enormous
cold	
	filthy
frightening	
	hilarious
good	
	boiling
interesting	
	amazing

9 Use the adjectives in Activity 8 in conversations with your partner.

Example: STUDENT A: *Tell me about something that's not just hot, but boiling.*

STUDENT B: *When I go clubbing, I'm boiling after a few dances.*

10 Listen to Track 11. What are the missing words?

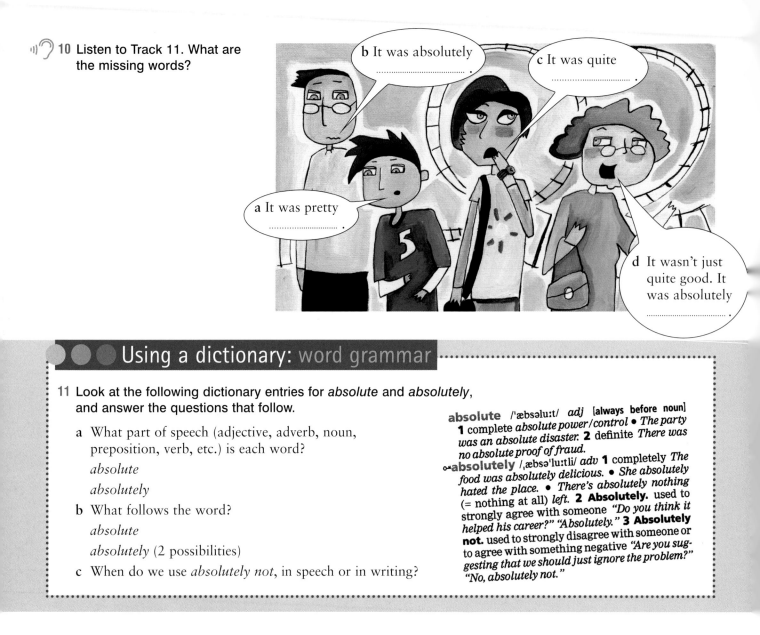

a It was pretty ....

b It was absolutely ....

c It was quite ....

d It wasn't just quite good. It was absolutely ....

Using a dictionary: word grammar

11 Look at the following dictionary entries for *absolute* and *absolutely*, and answer the questions that follow.

a What part of speech (adjective, adverb, noun, preposition, verb, etc.) is each word?

absolute

absolutely

b What follows the word?

absolute

absolutely (2 possibilities)

c When do we use *absolutely not*, in speech or in writing?

> **absolute** /ˈæbsəluːt/ *adj* [always before noun] **1** complete *absolute power/control* • *The party was an absolute disaster.* **2** definite *There was no absolute proof of fraud.*
> **absolutely** /ˌæbsəˈluːtli/ *adv* **1** completely *The food was absolutely delicious.* • *She absolutely hated the place.* • *There's absolutely nothing* (= nothing at all) *left.* **2 Absolutely.** used to strongly agree with someone *"Do you think it helped his career?" "Absolutely."* **3 Absolutely not.** used to strongly disagree with someone or to agree with something negative *"Are you suggesting that we should just ignore the problem?" "No, absolutely not."*

12 Look at how we can use adverbs before adjectives, and then do the exercise below.

ADVERB + ADJECTIVE

We can use adverbs (e.g. *fairly*, *really*) to make the meaning of an adjective stronger or weaker:

*It's **fairly** cold.*   *It's **really** cold.*

less than *very*	*very*	more than *very*
fairly	really	absolutely
quite		completely
rather		
pretty		

But note:
- we usually only use *absolutely* or *completely* with stronger adjectives; for example, we don't say ~~absolutely nice~~, but we do say *absolutely lovely*
- we don't use *very* with stronger adjectives because these adjectives already mean '*very*' for example, *furious* means *very angry*
- *pretty* is much more common in informal speech than in writing.

Put a cross [X] by the four adverb + adjective combinations that are <u>not</u> possible.

a pretty amazing   [ ]   e absolutely fascinating   [ ]   i very enormous   [ ]
b absolutely big   [ ]   f very boiling   [ ]   j quite fascinating   [ ]
c really terrifying   [ ]   g rather funny   [ ]
d very interesting   [ ]   h completely interesting   [ ]

13 Practice Imagine you are in some or all of the following situations. What's it like?

Example: STUDENT A: *You're about to give a speech to 500 people. What's that like?*

STUDENT B: *Absolutely terrifying.*

a You have to give a speech in front of 500 people.
b You are about to do a bungee jump off Sydney Harbour Bridge.
c You are about to do an exam.
d You're watching a comedy.

Functional language: giving opinions

14 Listen to Track 12 and complete the conversation.

A: Have you ever seen the original film of *Psycho*?
B: Yes.
A: ....
B: It was absolutely terrifying.
C: (Do) you really think so?
B: ....
C: No, not really. It's not my kind of film. I thought it was rather boring.

15 What phrase do the speakers use to:

a ... ask if something has happened?
b ... ask for opinions?
c ... give an opinion?

16 Is the following language used to agree or disagree with opinions? Put A (*Agree*) or D (*Disagree*) in the brackets.

a Do you really think so?   [D]
b I completely agree.   [   ]
c Yes it was, wasn't it?   [   ]
d I don't agree at all.   [   ]
e I don't think so.   [   ]
f You're absolutely right.   [   ]
g Yes. I thought so, too.   [   ]

17 Practice Copy and answer the following.

The last three films I have seen:
The last three good TV programmes I have seen:

Ask your partner about the films and programmes they have chosen.

Example: STUDENT A: *Have you seen 'Gone with the Wind'?*

STUDENT B: *No.*

STUDENT A: *Have you seen 'Casablanca'?*

STUDENT B: *Yes.*

STUDENT A: *What did you think of it?*

Grammar: past tenses

18 Write either the past simple or past continuous form of the verbs in brackets.

It (**a** be) ....was........ 6.15. In the Adelphi Theatre the actors (**b** arrive) .... for the evening performance. It (**c** raining) .... outside. Jack Long, the caretaker, (**d** sweep) .... the corridor when he (**e** hear) .... a loud voice. He (**f** look) .... around. On the stage a young woman (**g** stand) .... in the darkness, (**h** speak) .... loudly. When she (**i** notice) .... the caretaker, she (**j** stop) .... and (**k** run) .... off the stage. 'What (**l** you / do) ....?' he (**m** shout) .... The girl (**n** say) .... , 'I'm sorry. I (**o** pass) .... the theatre and the door (**p** is) .... open. I've never been on a stage before and I really (**q** want) .... to try it. I just want to be an actress!'

Look at 2A–2D in the Mini-grammar in the booklet for help.

19 Read the following story. Underline the past tense verbs in each sentence and circle the event that happened first.

a When David <u>got</u> home he <u>saw</u> that someone (had left) the front door open.

b He wondered what had happened.

c He noticed that someone had made a lot of footprints in the flowerbed.

d He was sure that he'd locked the door that morning.

e He was horrified to see that someone had smashed the window.

f David guessed that a burglar had broken in.

g He went into the sitting room and saw that the clock on the wall had gone.

h The burglar had not had time to take everything because David came home.

i When he had looked around the house he phoned the police.

j He told them exactly what the burglar had taken.

k The police said that he had done the right thing.

l He hadn't touched anything before he called them.

m They hoped that the damage had not been too serious.

n After he had finished the phone call he made himself a cup of tea.

o He was glad they hadn't taken the kettle!

Check your answers by looking at 2E and 2F in the Mini-grammar.

20 Look at the pictures. Which picture do the sentences below belong to?

a A man and a woman were walking, exhausted, in a desert. ......*picture 1*........

b But when they got there it had disappeared. ....

c He had taken off forty-five minutes earlier. ....

d He looked down and saw two people. ....

e He managed to land and helped the exhausted couple into his plane. ....

f It had been a mirage. ....

g Later that same day, towards evening, a pilot was flying his light aircraft low over the desert. ....

h Luckily they saw an oasis and hurried towards it. ....

i They had finished their water eight hours earlier / ago. ....

j They were collapsing and were clearly near to death. ....

Close your books and then see if you can tell the story from memory.

21 Role-play in groups of four: one person is a reporter and the other three are the pilot and the two walkers. Conduct a press interview about the story in Activity 20.

22 Read the newspaper report below and then answer these questions.

 a What saved someone?
 b Who was saved?
 c What was he saved from?

OVERALLS SAVE ABANDONED SAILOR

by Washington correspondent Anthony Dorking

A young US marine survived for nearly two days alone in the Arabian Sea, thanks to a pair of regulation overalls, according to the latest press release from the Pentagon.

Zachary Mayo, a 20-year-old lance corporal in the US Marines, woke up and couldn't get back to sleep. His cabin was too hot and stuffy. He got off his bunk quietly so as not to wake his shipmates. He put his blue overalls over his shorts and T-shirt he had been sleeping in, and left the cabin.

Zachary Mayo went up onto the deck of the USS America, a huge aircraft carrier. It was two o'clock on a Friday morning. He breathed in the fresh air and looked up at the stars in the clear night sky. And then, without thinking, he leaned out too far and lost his footing. Before he knew it, he was in the water, watching the huge ship disappearing into the night. Nobody had seen him fall, and for nearly two days not one of the 4,700 crew realised he had gone.

Mayo survived because at training camp two years before, he had been taught how to make clothes into life jackets. He took off his overalls and tied the arms and legs. Then he waved his 'life jacket' over his head and filled it with air so he could stay afloat. He did this many times during his ordeal.

After 34 hours, Mayo was sure he would die. He hadn't seen any search planes, and twice he had seen sharks swimming around him. Both nights that he was in the water he was attacked by smaller fish and he was slowly dying of thirst. Finally he fell asleep. When he woke up his overalls were floating away from him. In a fit of madness he tore off his T-shirt and shorts and prepared to die. And then, half an hour later, just before he lost consciousness, he saw a small boat.

A Pakistani fisherman, Abdul Aziz, was out in his boat that day. He couldn't believe his eyes when he saw Mayo's naked body, floating in the Arabian Sea, 100 miles from land. 'I thought it was a ghost!' he told reporters. But it was not a ghost. It was Zachary Mayo, and he was alive! But only just.

Two marines had been to see Mayo's parents in Osburn, Idaho, USA, to say that he was missing. His parents were desperately hoping for a miracle but they were almost sure that he was dead. They had to wait three days for news of his incredible rescue.

23 Read the text again and answer the following questions in your own words.

 a Why did Mayo go onto the deck?
 b How did he fall into the sea?
 c How did his overalls help him to survive?
 d Why did he think he was going to die?
 e Who talked to Mayo's parents, and what happened three days later?

24 Find words or phrases in the text, Activity 22, with the following meanings.

    a publicity and / or news given by an official organisation
    b the headquarters of the armed forces in the United States of America
    c airless, a feeling that it is difficult to breathe
    d a small bed often built above or below another bed, found in ships and in children's bedrooms
    e the surface that you walk on, on a ship
    f a ship that planes can land on and take off from
    g a terrible experience
    h a fantastic and amazing event

Language in chunks

25 Read the definitions and then complete the following phrases from the text in Activity 22.

    a to go to sleep again

       He couldn't get ....

    b he didn't think

       Without ....

    c to be unable to stand up, suddenly

       [Mayo] lost his ....

    d to behave in a crazy way for a moment

       In a fit ....

    e to stop being aware of the world

       just before he lost ....

    f to see something you can't believe

       Abdul Aziz couldn't believe ....

26 Use these phrases in sentences of your own.

27 **Noticing grammar** Find as many examples of *had* as you can in the text in Activity 22. Which are examples of the past perfect? Which are examples of another construction?

Speaking: telling stories

28 Look at the picture and answer the questions.

    a Where are Pete and Tabitha?
    b How are they feeling?
    c What do you think will happen next?

29 Work in pairs. Student A, look at Activity Bank 8 on page 153. Student B, look at Activity Bank 14 on page 156.

30 Work in pairs. Without looking back at the pictures, use the picture on this page and the other pictures you have seen to tell the story of Pete's and Tabitha's night out together.

Writing: headlines and newspapers

31 Look at the following headlines. What do you think the stories will be about?

Horrified driver sees attack

Turbulence terrifies teenager

Saved by sharp-eyed stewardess

Hero pulls neighbour from fire

Fuel gauge failure traps couple

32 Look at the headlines again and answer the following questions.

a Which kinds of word are commonly left out?
b Which kinds of words are included?
c What happens to the tense of the verbs?

33 Match the following stories with the headlines from Activity 31.

a A teenager flying from Istanbul to New York was absolutely terrified when the plane she was travelling in encountered major turbulence over the Atlantic.
  'We'd just had our meal when the pilot warned us about the weather,' said 16-year-old Gulay Menguç …

b A horrified car owner watched as youths attacked his car with bricks and a baseball bat. 'I had just come out of the house, when I saw this gang of youths. They were throwing things at my car and hitting it with a baseball bat …'

c How good is your eyesight? Could you see a burning ship from 35,000 feet? That's just what Julie did and today we say 'She's a hero!'
  Julie was working on a flight between Taipei and Sydney when she looked out of the window …

d A courageous villager battled through a burning bungalow to carry his neighbour to safety.
  Hero Laurence Broderick rescued Jean Buiter after a fire tore through her home in High Street, Waresly, destroying much of the roof.

e A frightened couple spent the night in their car in freezing temperatures after they ran out of fuel.
  'The gauge said we still had half a tank of petrol,' said Jane Bakewell after their ordeal, 'but then the car suddenly stopped and I had forgotten to bring my mobile phone with me, so …'

34 Fact check Answer these questions about the stories.

a Who was terrified where, after what?
b Who attacked what with what?
c Who saw what, from where?
d Who was saved from what, by whom, where?
e Who had forgotten what, and what effect did it have?

35 Write headlines to go at the beginning of these newspaper articles.

a A worker at Simpsons, the California meat packing company, was locked in a freezer cabinet all night when the door was closed while he was inside. 'It was so cold I nearly died,' he said, 'but I ran around all night and that kept me warm …'

b Two people were killed on Thursday when a large lorry crossed over the central section of the M40 motorway and smashed into a car. Police are investigating the incident.

c Fans of the band Warmheart were disappointed last night when their concert was cancelled. They were given tickets for the next concert tour in June.
  'We were very sorry,' said Warmheart's manager, 'but two of the band members, Ronnie and Chris, were very unwell. They just couldn't play. I nearly sent them to hospital.'

d A brave young girl is running a special marathon race in Bangkok tomorrow to raise money for cancer research.
  'My mother had cancer,' said Emma. 'She's better now, but I wanted to do something for people in the future.'
  Emma, who is 15 years old, has been training for two weeks. 'I'm nervous about the race,' she said. 'It's very long. But I'm going to raise a lot of money from my sponsors.'

Review: grammar and functional language

36 Read the following story and complete the tasks below.

Alison decided to go hill walking. She didn't tell anyone where she planned to go. When she reached the top of the first hill she looked for her map. She thought she had packed it in her jacket pocket, but it wasn't there. Suddenly a thick fog came down over the hills, and she couldn't see anything. She tried to find her way home, but she kept coming back to the same place. She was beginning to get very frightened. As she was stumbling along in the fog her foot went down a hole. It hurt terribly and she fainted. She had broken her ankle.

Back at home Alison's flatmate, Serena, was getting worried. It was dark and Alison still hadn't come home. Serena was afraid something had happened to her friend. At ten o'clock Serena rang the mountain rescue service.

When Alison woke up it was light and she was freezing cold. She realised she had been there all night. She heard a helicopter and she waved and shouted for help, but it was useless.

The search party didn't know where Alison had been. They had searched the whole area and they were exhausted. Just when they had decided to give up and go home, one of them saw a hand waving. It was Alison. She had crawled out of her hole and she was shouting for help. And the moral of the story? Don't forget your map when you go out alone and always tell someone where you are going.

  a Underline all the past tense verbs in the story.
  b How many past simple verbs are there?
  c How many past continuous verbs are there?
  d How many past perfect verbs are there?

37 Cover the text of the story in Activity 36. Write Alison's story in your own words without looking back at the text.

38 Complete the dialogue with one or more words for each gap.

  A: Have you (**a**) .... that film *Gladiator*? You know, the one they made years ago.

  B: Yes. It was (**b**) .... television the other day.

  A: What (**c**) .... of it?

  B: It was pretty good.

  A: Did you (**d**) .... ?

  B: Yes. Why? Didn't you?

  A: Not really. (**e**) .... really stupid – men running around killing each other, like that.

  B: Oh well, I don't (**f**) .... I enjoyed it.

  A: That's fine. It just isn't my kind (**g**) ...., that's all. But the one that's on at the ABC cinema – that's absolutely (**h**) .... I (**i**) .... loved it.

  B: You're joking, surely! I think it's (**j**) ....

  A: Terrible? Now you're joking!

Review: vocabulary

Word List

absolutely aircraft carrier amazing angry bad big boiling bunk claustrophobic cold deck dirty enormous fairly fantastic fascinating filthy freezing frightening funny furious garden shed good hilarious hot interesting ladder lawn (mower) lid miracle pirate pretty (adv) quite rather really shocked stuffy surprising terrible terrifying trapped trunk unconscious very water tank

Word Plus

a narrow escape
(I) couldn't believe (my) eyes
in a fit of madness
to get back to sleep
to lose consciousness
to lose your balance
without looking/thinking

39 Which words and phrases in the Word List do you already know?
Circle any 'new' words and look them up in a dictionary.
Write some sentences using them.

Pronunciation

40 Complete the following tasks.

a List the words from the Word List that you find easy to pronounce.
b Now list words from the Word List that you find the most difficult to pronounce.
Look at a dictionary to see how they should be said and practise saying them.
c Find all the words in the Word List with the letter 'a'. What is the most common pronunciation of the letter 'a' in these words?

Listen to Track 13 and check the pronunciation of the words in *c*.

41 Fill the circles below with adverbs and adjectives from the Word List.

adverbs	adjectives
absolutely	amazing

Work in pairs. Make sentences using an adverb and an adjective from the circles.
Are they correct? Your partner decides!

UNIT 3
What shoppers want

→ quantifiers with nouns
→ shopping collocations
→ asking for help in a store

Speaking: comparing opinions

1 **Discussion** Which of the following places to shop is best? Which is worst? Why?

a market   a supermarket   a shop   the internet

2 In pairs rewrite the following sentence so that it says what you both want it to say.

Men hate shopping, but women love it.

3 What about you? Do you like shopping? Choose the appropriate verb and complete the sentence. Compare what you have written with a partner.

I love / don't mind / hate shopping because …

Vocabulary: shopping collocations

●●● Using a dictionary: noun types

4 Look at the dictionary entry for *shopping* and answer these questions.

a Is *shopping* countable or uncountable?
b How do you know?
c What does '$' mean here?

> **shop·ping** [S2] [W3] /ˈʃɒpɪŋ $ ʃɑː-/ n [U]
> **1** the activity of going to shops and buying things: *Late-night shopping is becoming very popular.* | **shopping expedition/trip** *She's gone on a shopping trip to New York.* | *I went on a shopping spree* (=went shopping and bought a lot of things) *at the weekend and spent far too much money.* | *I've got to do some last-minute shopping.* | *the busy Christmas shopping season* → **WINDOW-SHOPPING**
> **2 do the shopping** to go shopping to buy food and oth...

5 The words in the box can be used together with *shopping*.
Can you put them in the right place in the table?

trolley	late-night
centre	bag
complex	list
do the	malls
expedition	serious
go	Sunday
Internet	window-
last-minute	

a *shopping* + noun (to create a new compound noun)	**b** adjective / noun / verb } + *shopping*
shopping trolley	

6 Use the *shopping* phrases from Activity 5 to complete what you think these people are saying.

a I've still got some

....

to do before the party tomorrow.

b I don't really need to buy anything. I'm just

....

to see what the new fashions are like.

c I prefer to do all my shopping at a .... because everything you need is there, and there's usually somewhere to have a coffee when you've finished.

d How do you fancy a really good

.... ?

We could stay in town for the whole day.

e I don't agree with

....

We should have one day when everyone can relax.

f Excuse me, sir, where did you get this

.... ?

Now listen to Track 14. Were you correct?

7 Discussion Ask your partner to tell you about the last time they went shopping. Find out where they went, how they felt about it and what they went to buy. Did they enjoy it?

Reading: at the supermarket

8 Creative task Work in pairs. On the supermarket plan choose the best place for:

- ... the products you want to sell most
- ... drinks
- ... the meat and fish counter
- ... fruit and vegetables

Write in the names of the products where you think they should be.

Think about what sort of colours, smells, lighting and noises there might be in the supermarket. Make a note of your ideas below.

- smells: ....

....

- colours: ....

....

- lighting: ....

....

- noises: ....

....

9 Read the text below. Is your supermarket plan, in Activity 8, similar to this?

Few shoppers go to the supermarket with lists, so supermarkets want to encourage them to buy a lot of **everything**. How do they do this?

○ The entrance is normally at one side and the exit at the other so that shoppers walk down all the aisles before leaving.

○ Fruit and vegetables are normally close to the entrance. This makes people think they are going into an open-air market and makes them feel positive.

○ Meat and fish counters are usually placed on the back wall. Supermarkets do not want to risk putting off their customers by taking meat carcasses through the shop.

○ Some shelf spaces are better than others! The middle shelves on the left are considered the best place. Suppliers sometimes pay supermarkets for the best places!

○ Vacuum-packed meats and fish look clean and bloodless. When you buy your lamb chops you are thinking of convenience and availability rather than a lamb in the field.

○ Stores are usually decorated in colours that make people feel healthy and happy. All the supermarkets belonging to one company have the same colours to make people feel at home.

○ A person blinks an average of 32 times a minute. US research has shown that a certain type of lighting can reduce this to 14 times a minute. This can make customers feel sleepy, and they then buy more goods.

○ Goods placed at the end of an aisle often sell five times more than those placed in the middle of the aisle. Stores often move goods that they particularly want to sell, such as those nearing their sell-by date, to these sites.

○ Supermarkets try to control smells. Unpleasant aromas, such as those of fish, are taken away by air extractors. Fresh smells, such as baking bread, may be pumped around the store to create a nice 'homely' feel.

○ Most shoppers buy bread, so the bakery counter is situated as far away from the entrance as possible. Customers will have to walk past hundreds of other products to reach it.

○ Drinks are usually located near the exit. Supermarkets hope that customers will buy because they are in a good mood as they finish their shopping experience.

○ Silence makes shoppers feel uncomfortable. Supermarkets like to make sure that there is quite a lot of pleasant background noise, such as music or the hum of freezers.

○ Security cameras are not just for catching shoplifters. Supermarkets also follow a few shoppers through the shop so that they can observe what routes people take. This information helps them to rearrange their products so that people buy more.

10 Fact check Are the following facts *True* or *False* according to the text? Give reasons for your choice.

a People go to supermarkets with a clear idea of what they are going to buy.
b Shoppers like the sight of fresh fruit and vegetables.
c Meat counters are usually near the front of a supermarket.
d The goods on the top shelves always sell the best.
e Supermarkets still don't know what colours relax people.
f Sleepy people buy less than people who are awake.
g People are influenced by what they can smell.
h Shoppers like silence.

11 Vocabulary Find words in the text with the following meanings. The first letter of each word is given.

a passageway between two rows of shelves: (a)
b outside: (o-a)
c the remains of dead animals: (c)
d in a see-through container with the air removed: (v-p)
e to open and shut your eyes very quickly: (b)
f the last day on which you can buy something: (s-b, d)
g a continuous sound which is not very loud: (b, n)
h watch: (o)

Language in chunks

12 In the text in Activity 9, find at least four examples of the phrase *make* (*someone*) *feel* (*something*).

13 Find out from your classmates what makes them feel:

> angry   excited   happy   nervous   positive   relaxed   sad   sleepy

Example: STUDENT A: *What makes you feel happy?*

STUDENT B: *Lots of things: nice food, friends, sunny days.*

14 Which of these sentences summarise the text best? Talk to your neighbour.
Can you write a better summary?

a Supermarkets try to trick customers into buying products that they don't want. This is a bad thing.
b Supermarkets try to make shopping pleasant for their customers. This is a good thing.

What do you think of the information you have read? Compare your reactions with a partner.

Grammar: quantifiers

15 Put the following quantifiers in the right place on the scale.

> a few   a little   a lot of   every   many   most   not much / many   several   some

0% |··| 100%
not any   **all**

16 Choose the correct quantifiers in the following sentences.

a Some / Much shops open on a Sunday.
b I don't get much / many pleasure from shopping – in fact, I hate it!
c I usually eat some / several fruit for lunch.
d I have a beer all / every lunchtime.
e I often sleep for a few / a little minutes after lunch.
f A lot of / Every people eat out at restaurants.
g He always puts a lot of / many sugar in his coffee.
h When I go to the supermarket, I always buy a little / a few cheese.

Look at 3A–3F in the Mini-grammar to check your answers.

17 Look at the following sentences about shopping in Britain.
Add a quantifier from the explanations above according to the
quantity indicated on the right.

a ......*Most*...... people shop in supermarkets.
b .... goods are sold cheaply to make sure people
   buy them.
c .... families go shopping on Sundays.
d .... people buy things in small village shops
   nowadays.
e Not .... shoplifters get sent to prison.
f .... supermarket companies try to improve the areas
   they build in.
g .... supermarkets offer very little choice.
h Some prices are reduced .... Saturday afternoon.

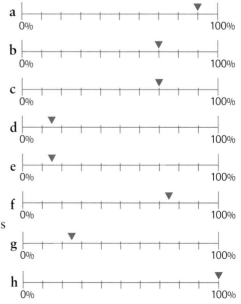

18 Work in pairs. Change these statements using quantifiers so that they reflect your point of view.

Example: *Boys like football.*

It's true that a lot of boys like football, but not all of them do. A few aren't interested at all.

a Girls are interested in fashion
b Young people like discos.
c Young people don't like school.
d People think films are more interesting than plays at the theatre.
e Old people watch television every evening.

Functional language: going shopping

19 Before you listen to Track 15, put the following lines (*1–4*) in the right places in the conversations below.

1 Do you know where I could find some?
2 They might be able to help.
3 They're over there by those shirts.
4 Let me know if I can help you with anything.

GARY: Can I help you?
KYLIE: No thanks. I'm just looking around.
GARY: OK.

(**a**) ....

....

KYLIE: Thanks.
GARY: No problem.

ANDY: Excuse me.
GARY: Yes. How can I help you?
ANDY: I'm looking for Takez jeans.
GARY: I'm afraid we don't sell Takez.
ANDY: Oh, that's a pity.

(**b**) ....

GARY: Well, you could try the shop on the corner.

(**c**) ....

ANDY: Thanks.
GARY: You're welcome.

POLLY: Excuse me. Do you have any belts?
GARY: Yes we do.

(**d**) ....

....

POLLY: Oh yes, so they are. Thanks.

Now listen to track 15. Were you correct?

20 Look at the following list of clothes. Tick the words you know.

belt	[ ]	jeans	[ ]	sweater	[ ]	fleece	[ ]
dress	[ ]	shirt	[ ]	(a pair of) trousers	[ ]	sandals	[ ]
gloves	[ ]	skirt	[ ]	T-shirt	[ ]	shorts	[ ]
hat	[ ]	socks	[ ]	cap	[ ]	(a pair of) tights	[ ]

Find out the meaning of the words you didn't tick by using a dictionary.

● ● ● Pronunciation: same sound

21 Find words which share a vowel sound on their stressed syllable. Join them together.

anything   belt

cap   dress   every   fleece   gloves

hat   help   jeans   many   much   several

shirt   skirt   some   sweater   T-shirt

welcome   please

Listen to Track 16 to check your answers.

22 Who's wearing what? Ask your partner about the clothes and the people.

Example: STUDENT A: *Who's wearing shorts?*

STUDENT B: *Charlene is.*

Complete these sentences.

a Barbara's wearing *a dress, a sweater and boots. And she's got a hat on too.*

b Charlene's wearing ....

c Donald's wearing ....

d Phoebe's wearing ....

e Margaret's wearing ....

f Ashley's wearing ....

Barbara   Charlene   Donald   Phoebe   Margaret   Ashley

23 Role-play Work in pairs. One of you works in a clothes shop, the other is a customer. Role-play conversations using language from Activities 19 and 20.

Listening: radio commercials

24 Listen to the radio commercials on Track 17. Which is the odd one out (*1, 2, 3,* or *4*)? Why?

25 Match the commercials *1–4* with these pictures.

26 Listen to Track 17 again. Answer these questions.

    a 500 what?
    b We're here to help you with what?
    c 400 what for what?
    d 350 what for what?
    e One in three what?
    f Don't kid who?
    g Kill what?
    h Hate what?
    i Book your holidays from where?

27 Which is the best commercial? Why? Does everyone agree?

28 Complete the following phrases from the radio commercials.

    a Help is ....
    b Just one of the .... we've got for you.
    c .... at any branch ...
    d Announcing the great Furniture Fanfare ....
    e We've got everything .... at prices
    ....
    f .... is the click of a mouse.
    g The place everyone ....

29 Creative task You are going to write a radio commercial for a product.

    a Choose one of the following products or think of your own:

        car   chocolate bar   mobile phone   pair of trainers   computer game   fizzy / soft drink

    b Complete the following table.

What is the product?	
What are its main selling points (price, what's special about it, convenience, etc.)?	
Describe the characters and situation for the commercial (e.g. two men in a lift, two women in a café).	
What is the 'punchline' (e.g. *We're here to help you with all those numbers.*)?	
What music and / or sound effects will you use in the commercial?	

    c Now write your commercial. You can use language from Activity 28 or
    from the Audioscript for Track 17 in the booklet at the back.
    Record your commercial onto a tape. Does it sound good?

Writing: paragraph construction

30 Read the paragraph. What information is given about:

a ... some people?
b ... a lot of things?
c ... the majority of people?
d ... many people?

Some people think that the Internet has changed the way that people in rich countries shop. It is certainly possible to buy a lot of things now – from groceries to books – without leaving the house. But other commentators think that the majority of people would still rather go to a shop or supermarket with real people in it than log on to a website. There is no doubt, however, that computers have had an impact on the shopping habits of many people.

31 Discussion Have you ever bought anything on the Internet? Is it better than going to a shop? Why?

32 Think about the structure of a paragraph like the one above. It is often made up of the following types of sentence:

a an introductory sentence
b an example or explanation sentence
c an exception or question sentence
d a conclusion

What type of sentence (a–d in the list above):

1 ... closes the paragraph?
2 ... contrasts with the introductory sentence?
3 ... follows on from the introductory sentence, expanding on the information in it?
4 ... introduces the subject matter of the paragraph?

33 Can you identify the different types of sentence in the paragraph in Activity 30?

34 Put the following sentences in order to make a paragraph.

a In it she suggests that buying things helps the world's economy and allows us all to take part in social life.
b *Point of Purchase*, a new book by Sharon Zukin, shows the incredible impact that shopping has had on modern life.
c *Point of Purchase* is a fascinating read which tells a fantastic story of how human beings try to make their lives better.
d She doesn't condemn our consumer-minded society, as some writers do, but instead she explores the reasons why shopping is so important in our lives.

35 Writing Write a four-sentence paragraph about one of the following.

a The Internet is a threat to traditional shopping.
b Shoplifting is not such a serious crime.
c Shopping centres are killing off small local shops.
d Advertising should be banned.

Review: grammar and functional language

36 Look at the results of a survey about what people have for breakfast. Complete the sentences using the information in the survey.

Example: *Not many people drink milk for breakfast.*

What people drink:	What people eat:
44% tea	51% cereal (cornflakes, muesli)
41% coffee	23% toast
7% fruit juice	15% cooked breakfasts (fried bacon, egg, sausage)
3% milk	7% no breakfast
3% water	4% boiled eggs
2% nothing	

37 What do people have for breakfast in your country? Make statements.

Example: *Not many people drink tea at breakfast in my country.*

38 Complete the following sentences in any way you want.

a Some people think that

....

b I spend most of my free time

....

c Very few of my friends

....

d There's little chance of

....

e It only takes a few minutes to

....

f Before I saw one in an advertisement, I had never

....

39 Work in pairs. Write a new conversation in which a customer goes into a clothes shop and either asks for help or is offered help by the shop assistant.

Mime your conversation for the class. Can they work out what your original conversation was?

Review: vocabulary

Word List

aisle   background noise   belt   blink   cap   carcass
commercial   fleece   gloves   hat
Internet shopping   jeans   last-minute shopping   late-night shopping
market   observe   open-air   sandals   sell-by date   serious shopping
shirt   shopping bag   shopping centre   shopping complex
shopping expedition   shopping list   shopping mall   shopping spree
shopping trolley   shorts   skirt   socks   Sunday shopping
supermarket   sweater   tights   trousers   T-shirt   vacuum-packed
window-shopping

Word Plus

at affordable prices
all it takes is ...
help is at hand
to do the / my shopping
to go shopping
to make someone feel
   angry / excited / happy etc.
to put somebody off

40 Group the words in the Word List into different meaning groups (such as clothing, places, etc.).
How many meaning groups are there? Are there any words that don't fit any groups?
Compare your lists with a partner's.

◯ ● ● Pronunciation

41 a Write down pairs of words from the Word List with the same vowel sound (e.g. *cap / hat*).

  ))) Listen to Track 18 and check.

  b Which words in the list have the same sound /ʃ/ as *shopping*?

  ))) Listen to Track 19 and check.

42 Write five sentences with gaps to test your partner's knowledge of words and phrases
from the Word List and Word Plus. Then give your partner the sentences to complete.

Example: I usually .... my shopping on Saturday mornings.
         (I usually do my shopping on Saturday mornings.)

43 Writing Work in pairs. Invent a story on one of the following topics.

  a My worst ever shopping experience
  b My best ever shopping experience
  c The time I went shopping and met ...
  d I'm never going shopping again because ...

Listening: holiday preferences

1 **Discussion** Choose one of the following pictures. Tell a partner why it is the best type of holiday to go on.

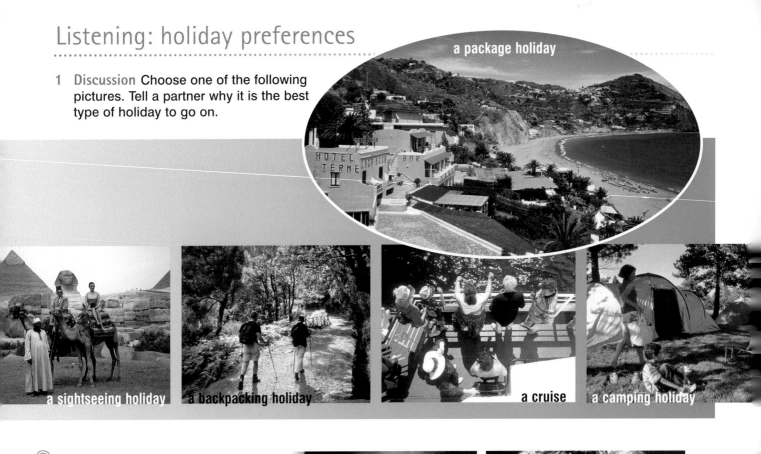

a package holiday

a sightseeing holiday

a backpacking holiday

a cruise

a camping holiday

2 Before you listen to Track 20, look at the five people in these pictures. Who likes which type of holiday, shown in Activity 1, do you think?

Tony

Sandra

Meera

Josette

Steve

Now listen to Track 20. Were you correct?

3 Look at the dictionary entries for *holiday, holidaymaker* and *vacation*. Answer the questions which follow.

a Which words can be both a noun and a verb in:
... American English?
... British English?
How do you know?

b In American English, which word can be used for the time when students are not studying?
How do you know?

c Which speakers use the word *holidaymaker*?
Which speakers use the word *vacationer*?
How do you know?

d Using your own dictionary, find at least two more examples where American and British English have different words for the same thing.

hol·i·day² *v* [I] *BrE* to spend your holiday in a place – used especially in news reports; ⊟ **vacation** *AmE*: [+**in/at**] *They're holidaying in Majorca.*

hol·i·day·mak·er /ˈhɒlɪdi,meɪkə $ ˈhɑːlɪdeɪ,meɪkər/ *n* [C] *BrE* someone who has travelled to a place on holiday; → **tourist**; ⊟ **vacationer** *AmE*

va·ca·tion¹ [S2] [W3] /vəˈkeɪʃən $ veɪ-/ *n*
1 [C,U] *especially AmE* a holiday, or time spent not working

vacation² *v* [I] *AmE* to go somewhere for a holiday: [+**in/at**] *The Bernsteins are vacationing in Europe.*

hol·i·day¹ [S2] [W2] /ˈhɒlɪdi, -deɪ $ ˈhɑːlɪdeɪ/ *n*
1 [C,U] *BrE* also **holidays** a time of rest from work, school etc; ⊟ **vacation** *AmE*: *The school holidays start tomorrow.* | **on holiday** *I'm away on holiday until the 1st of June.* | *Won't your business suffer if you **take** a holiday?*

4 **Fact check** Listen to Track 20 again. Who:

a ... doesn't like tourist resorts?
b ... has tried water skiing?
c ... loves a bit of luxury?
d ... has children who go swimming and boating?
e ... doesn't sunbathe?
f ... has been to Scotland?
g ... likes nightlife and clubbing?
h ... likes places off the beaten track?
i ... likes galleries and museums?

5 **Vocabulary** Use the diagram as a start for your own holiday 'wordmap'.
Use words from Activities 1–4. You can also look at the Audioscript for Track 20 to find more holiday words. How many more words can you add to the 'wordmap'?

sun   sea

package holiday

nightlife   holiday

camping

campsite   tent

Reading: welcome to Backpackerland!

6 Read the report on 'Backpackerland'. Which of the following statements best sums it up?

a Backpackerland is in Australia.
b Backpackerland is a name for any place where a certain kind of traveller goes.
c Backpackerland is the name of a kind of clothing.
d Backpackerland is a type of cybercafé.

Once you've left the airport you find yourself a cheap hostel and sleep badly because it's hot, much hotter than it was when you left home, and you haven't paid enough for an air-conditioned room. Besides, there's the noise of the busy street and some crazy tourist playing a harmonica all night. On top of that you're jet-lagged because you've crossed two time zones at least. All your worst nightmares have come true, but you don't care, because this is an adventure and you aren't at home any more.

In the morning you feel exhausted but more alive than you have for years. You go out on to the street and have your first cup of coffee. Everywhere there are foreign vehicles, strange smells, different colours and people wearing different clothes. As you look up and down the street you see more and more people just like yourself, travellers – but they've been here for at least three days. They're much more interesting-looking than you, and seem completely at home as they visit the shops and market stalls, or hurry into the cybercafés to see if their mums have sent them an email. Welcome to Backpackerland.

Backpackerland is a new world of possibility, not quite real. You go into it as a third-year economics student from Liverpool, a young lawyer from Seattle, a secretary from Melbourne or a student teacher from Turin. A few dollars later you are a cross between a 19th-century adventurer, a 20th-century clubber and a 21st-century philosopher reading travel guides and writing poetry by the roadside.

Backpackerland has recognised meeting points like Khao San Road in Bangkok, the Kings Cross area of Sydney, and the Colaba Causeway in India. It exists because travel is cheaper than ever before. Each year, more and more young people cross the world from east to west, from north to south, stuffing clothes, notebooks and

Peter Hedley on the modern way to travel – for some!

cameras into their backpacks to experience the clamour of Mexico City, the heat of the Atacama desert or the snowy altitudes of Nepal.

Travelling has changed out of all recognition in the last 30 years. In the old days you waited for months for a letter from your granny and if you ever did manage to phone home it cost the earth and you couldn't hear each other properly. It was only the bravest who risked cutting themselves off like that. Now you're almost never out of touch. The cybercafé computers in Kathmandu, Phnom Penh and La Paz are as fast as anything you'll find in Tokyo, Washington or Berlin. So the moment you get off the plane you can email the friend you had a drink with the day before you left home.

When I was last in Thailand I bumped into Colin, the man who'd done the electric wiring in my little flat in London. Back home he'd always seemed miserable and cold, but now Colin (who had just been exploring in the jungle) was tanned and fit, and he was smiling a lot. That's the kind of thing that happens in Backpackerland. You can be anyone you want to be and life is full of surprises.

7 Fact check Read the text again and answer the following questions.

a How old are most backpackers?
b What occupations do backpackers have?
c Are they rich or poor?
d Why does Backpackerland exist now?
e How can holidaymakers communicate with each other and with people at home when they are travelling?

8 Vocabulary Find words or phrases in the text with the following meanings.

a a small cheap hotel (paragraph 1)
b mechanically cooled (paragraph 1)
c tired because you've travelled across the world on a plane (paragraph 1)
d places with computers which anyone can pay to use (paragraph 2)
e places where you can buy things – the places are often smaller than a shop, and usually in the open air (paragraph 2)
f books specially for travellers (paragraph 3)
g noise and bustle (paragraph 4)
h people with the most courage (paragraph 5)

9 Noticing language How many examples of comparative and superlative adjectives can you find in the text? Create sentences using these adjectives.

Language in chunks

10 Complete these phrases from the text using the words in the box.

| at home | between (X and Y) | of surprises |
| of touch | the earth | |

a a cross ....
b completely ....
c cost ....
d life is full ....
e out ....

11 Complete the sentences with the completed phrases from Activity 10.

a With a mobile phone you're never ....
b I never thought I'd visit Italy again. ....
c She relaxes a lot when she gets here. She feels ....
d I don't know what it is. It looks like .... a bicycle and a car.
e Her engagement ring had three huge diamonds. It ....

12 Discussion Work in pairs. Ask and answer the following questions.

a Have you ever been a backpacker? (If your partner's answer is 'yes', find out as much information as you can.)
b Would you like to be a backpacker? Why? Why not?
c Where would you most like to go as a backpacker?

Speaking: a debate

13 Creative task You are going to have a TV debate on the following topic.

Tourism: a good thing for us all?

a Work in groups. Group A: how many reasons can you think of why tourism might be a bad thing? Look at Activity Bank 9 on page 153 for more arguments. Group B: how many reasons can you think of why tourism might be a good thing? Look at Activity Bank 15 on page 156 for more arguments.

b Elect a member of the class to be the TV host. The host will be in charge of the debate. Everyone else: choose one of the following roles for yourself in the TV debate and be prepared to argue either for or against tourism from that person's viewpoint.

airline executive	hotel employee
travel writer	fisherman
environmentalist	politician
holidaymaker	travel agent

c Have the debate. The host starts the programme.

Grammar: comparative and superlative adjectives

14 Look at the pictures of the three hotels and compare them, using comparative and superlative forms of the adjectives in the box, plus any other adjectives you can think of.

> attractive   beautiful   big   cheap   comfortable   crazy   crowded   exciting   expensive   interesting
> large   lively   luxurious   modern   noisy   old   old-fashioned   peaceful   quiet   relaxing

Check your answers by looking at **4A and 4B in the Mini-grammar**.

15 Complete the following exchanges with the phrases in the box.

> a bit more difficult   and more exciting   as he is   hotter and hotter   as much as
> much more interesting   the better   the bigger   the easiest   less than

a 'Why are you going inside?'
'It's getting *hotter and hotter* ! I can't stand it.'

b 'You seem to be enjoying that book.'
'Yes. It's .... than I had expected.'

c 'When are you going to finish putting up those shelves?'
'As soon as I can. It's .... than I expected.'

d 'You can't hear yourself speak in here.'
'Great! The noisier ....'

e 'You don't want coffee? I thought you liked coffee.'
'Not .... I used to.'

f 'Why don't you want to play cards with your brother?'
'I'm not as good at cards ....'

g 'The meals here are absolutely enormous.'
'Great! .... the better!'

h 'Isn't it all too expensive?'
'Oh no. You can get a flight for .... £65.'

i 'How did you get on in the exam?'
'Great. It was .... one of all of them.'

j 'Why are you so keen on that television programme?'
'Because it's getting more ....'

Check your answers by looking at **4C in the Mini-grammar**.

16 Practice Use language from Activities 14 and 15 to compare one of the following.

a Two holiday destinations in your country which are very different.

b Two holiday destinations in the world that you know about, have seen pictures of, or have visited.

c Holidaying today compared to holidaying 50 years ago.

Functional language: recommendations

17 Before you listen to Track 21, put the travel agent's questions and recommendations (in the box) into the correct gaps to complete the conversation.

TRAVEL AGENT: **(a)** ....

BEN: We'd like to book a holiday.

DUNCAN: Yes, can you recommend anything?

TRAVEL AGENT: **(b)** ....

DUNCAN: Oh you know, sun, sea, sand, the usual.

TRAVEL AGENT: **(c)** ....

BEN: Well, we've been to Spain once already.

TRAVEL AGENT: **(d)** ....

DUNCAN: Italy? That's a great idea, but actually we'd prefer somewhere a bit more, well, exotic.

TRAVEL AGENT: **(e)** ....

BEN: I don't think we could afford that.

TRAVEL AGENT: **(f)** ....

DUNCAN: Yes, but is it worth it?

TRAVEL AGENT: **(g)** ....

BEN: Can I have a look at the brochure?

TRAVEL AGENT: **(h)** ....

BEN: Thanks.

○ Actually, it's probably not as expensive as you think.

○ All right then, can I suggest Rio de Janeiro?

○ OK, what about somewhere in Spain, say Sitges near Barcelona?

○ Sure. Take your time.

○ Well, it's definitely worth considering.

○ Well, what kind of holiday do you want?

○ Well then, how about Sorrento in Italy?

○ Yes, can I help you?

Now listen to Track 21. Were you correct?

18 Look at how we can ask for and give recommendations.

ASKING FOR AND GIVING RECOMMENDATIONS

1 We can ask for recommendations like this:
Can you recommend somewhere to stay near the sea?
Can you suggest a good place for a holiday?
Have you got any ideas about a good hotel?
Is it worth { *visiting Wellington?*
{ *seeing Auckland?*
Is Paris worth { *a visit?*
{ *considering?*

2 We can make recommendations like this:
What about (going to) Alaska?
How about the Hotel Stella?
Have you thought of (going to) London?
Why don't you try somewhere in Portugal?
If it was me, I'd go somewhere cheaper.
Why don't you give it a try?

3 We can reply to recommendations like this:
That sounds like a great idea!
That's exactly what I was looking for.
That's not quite what { *I was looking for.*
{ *I was thinking of.*
That's a great idea, but I'd rather go somewhere more comfortable.
I think we'd prefer something a bit less expensive.

19 Make new questions and sentences by replacing the blue words, in Activity 18, with words of your own. Here are some examples:

Can you recommend somewhere with really good sports facilities?

If it was me, I'd go somewhere more beautiful.

20 Work in pairs. Use the language from Activity 18 to ask for and give recommendations in three of the following situations.

   a You go to a travel agent to ask about how to travel from one place to another.

   b On a trip abroad you ask the hotel receptionist about which plays and / or restaurants to go to.

   c A customer doesn't know which dish to choose in a restaurant.

   d A friend doesn't know what to buy a girlfriend / boyfriend for a Valentine's Day present.

   e A customer in a shop doesn't know which dress / shirt to buy.

● ● ● Pronunciation: pitch and intonation

21 Listen to people accepting recommendations on Track 22. Are they really enthusiastic or not?

   a That sounds fantastic.

   b That sounds like a great idea.

   c That's exactly what I want.

   d That's just right.

   e That's incredible.

   f That's a great suggestion.

22 Say the sentences using the same pitch and intonation as the speakers.

23 **Role-play** Work in pairs. Imagine you are travel agents. Think about the kinds of holidays you have to offer. Copy and complete the tables in Activity bBank 4 on page 152.

Now find a different partner. One of you wants to go on holiday. The other is the travel agent. The holidaymaker should ask the travel agent for advice and listen to the information carefully before deciding where to go. Once you have finished, swap roles.

Writing: coherence and cohesion

24 Choose a public holiday in your country. Make notes to show how you would explain it to a foreign visitor. Explain:

   a ... when it is.

   b ... what it's for.

   c ... what special customs or events happen on that day.

   d ... what you usually do on that day.

25 Look at the pictures. Do you know what the two festivals are? Put the paragraphs on the right in the correct order. (The first paragraph is *d*.)

a Many national festivals have been celebrated for years, but occasionally new ones come along and old ones gradually disappear. This is unlikely to happen to Burns' Night or St Patrick's Day, however. They are celebrated by too many people for that.

b On Burns' Night the guests eat haggis. Haggis is chopped mutton and other ingredients – including liver, heart and oats – encased in sheep's gut, which is boiled before being served. The haggis is brought into the room to the sound of the bagpipes and the chief guest 'addresses' it, reciting Burns' poem 'Ode to the Haggis'. After eating, the other guests recite more of Burns' poems, sing Scottish tunes and drink a lot of whisky.

c On St Patrick's Day there are big parades, and people wear shamrocks. In some places they add green colouring to the beer and even to rivers and streams. People go out and have 'a good craic' (pronounced 'crack') – Irish for good fun.

d Public holidays and festivals are an important part of a country's life. They give everyone a break from routine and they form part of the annual life in that country. Sometimes they celebrate a day in a country's history (Independence Day), commemorate a special person (Columbus Day), mark the passing of time (New Year's Day) or celebrate a religious festival (Christmas, Eid, Diwali).

e Another widely celebrated festival is St Patrick's Day (17 March), which celebrates the life of the 5th-century saint. St Patrick was Bishop of Ireland, and it is said that he gave Ireland its national symbol when he illustrated his religious teaching with the shamrock – a three-leafed clover. But the festival is now more than anything a celebration of 'Irishness', whether it takes place in Dublin, Auckland, Melbourne, Montreal or Boston.

f Two particular festivals are celebrated far beyond their native land. The first of these, Burns' Night on 25 January, marks the birthday of the Scottish poet Robert Burns (1759–96). It is celebrated by his countrymen and admirers, not only in Scotland but all over the world, from New York to Sydney, from Toronto to Tokyo.

26 Fact check Who or what is:

a ... Robert Burns?
b ... a haggis?
c ... the Ode to the Haggis?
d ... St Patrick?
e ... a shamrock?
f ... 'a good craic'?

27 Look at the notes you made for Activity 24. Use them to write an article based on the plan on the right.

Paragraph 1:
Introduce the topic.
↓

Paragraph 2:
Give details to illustrate and expand the facts / opinions from the introductory paragraph.
↓

Paragraphs 3, 4, 5, 6, etc: Give further examples that either add to or contrast with the previous paragraphs.
↓

Conclusion:
Either make a general comment, **or** summarise the contents of the previous paragraphs **or** make predictions about the future.

Review: grammar and functional language

28 Match the questions and answers.

a Can you recommend a good holiday destination?
b Do you like going on cruises?
c Do you want to come pony-trekking with us?
d Have you thought of going to the Costa del Sol?
e What's the most exciting thing you've ever done?
f What's your favourite kind of holiday resort?
g Which do you prefer: galleries or museums?

1 Neither really. They're both as boring as each other.
2 No, thanks. At ninety years old I'm not as energetic as I was.
3 Oh, definitely the noisier the better.
4 That's a great idea, but I think I'd prefer somewhere a bit more exotic.
5 The parachute jump I did last year, I think.
6 Well, have you thought of going to South America?
7 Yes, because the ships are getting better and better.

Ask your partner the same questions. Do they give different answers?

29 Have a quiz. In teams of about four people, write questions about world geography and world landmarks.

Example: *Which is the longest river in the world?*

Take it in turns to ask the other team(s) questions. Your team gets one point for giving a correct answer.

30 Writing Look at the picture.

Imagine you are encouraging someone to:
a ... buy a diamond in a jewellery store.
b ... look at the inside of their car engine.
c ... do a bungee jump.
d ... eat fried ants.
e ... take a ride on a rollercoaster.

Make sentences for the different situations. Use the words in the box and the pattern *Don't worry. It's not as ... as it looks / seems / sounds.*

Are my boy's injuries really serious?

Don't worry, sir. It's not as bad as it looks.

bad   dangerous   expensive   frightening   complicated
boring   disgusting   terrifying   uncomfortable

Review: vocabulary

Word List

abroad   air-conditioned   backpacking   camping   campsite
clamour   clubbing   cruise   cybercafé   environmentalist
excursion   festival   gallery   holiday   holidaymaker   hostel
jet-lagged   market stalls   museum   nightlife   package holiday
pony-trekking   public holiday   resort   sightseeing   sunbathe
tanned   tourist   travel guide   vacation   waterski (v)

Word Plus

Life is full of surprises.
a cross between (X) and (Y)
off the beaten track
to be completely at home
to be out of touch
to cost the earth

31 Imagine you are going to be stranded on a desert island and you can only take five words from the Word List with you. Which ones will you take and why?

Example: I'll take 'pony-trekking' because I like the sound of it – and I could get around the island more easily.

🔘🔘⚫ Pronunciation

32 a How many words can you find in the Word list which have the sound /æ/ – like *cat*?

Listen to Track 23 and check.

b Find the odd one out in the following lists.

Think about sounds.

1 package   vacation   backpacking   camping   fantastic
2 clubbing   cruise   public   sunbathe   fun

Think about syllables.

3 backpacking   boating   excursion   holiday   waterski
4 camping   culture   hostel   abroad   museum
   sunbathe

Think about stress.

5 gallery   nightlife   sunbathe   resort   swimming
6 holiday   gallery   excursion   sightseeing   luxury

Listen to Track 24 and check.

33 Speaking Imagine that you are a journalist who works for a television travel programme. Write six questions you would always ask about any travel destination. Ask about local sites, activities, atmosphere, the weather, etc.

In pairs, role-play a conversation between the journalist and a local resident. The journalist starts by asking one of the prepared questions.

UNIT 5

Home

→ present perfect
→ homes and houses
→ welcoming people to your home

Speaking: where I live (game)

1 Look at these words in the box below and find pairs of words with opposite meanings.

> bare cold cramped cluttered
> light untidy spacious tidy
> dark warm

2 Choose one of the homes in the picture.

Using words from Activity 1 and any other words you know, list the advantages and disadvantages of the home you have chosen. Here is an example:

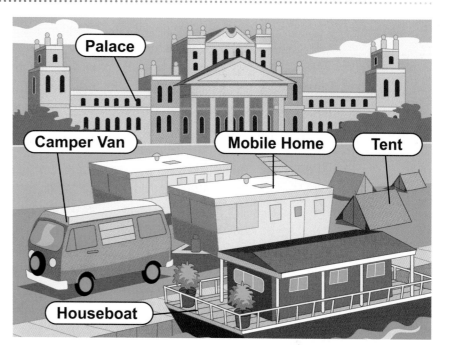

Your choice: ......tent.............	
Advantages:	Disadvantages:
light, easy to carry	uncomfortable, cold

3 Without saying which home you have chosen, tell the rest of the class about its advantages and disadvantages. The class has to guess which home it is.

Reading: a different kind of home

4 Read the text on the next page. Some sentences are missing. Where do the following sentences *a–f* go in the text on page 46? The first one is done for you.

a Since I started living in my van, I've had feelings I haven't experienced since I was a child. **4**

b I was trying to decide what to do when I saw the advertisement: 'Converted ambulance for sale, £1,600'.

c Now I begin to appreciate what travellers have been telling us all these years.

d One problem I've had is what to do about power for my computer.

e Parking can be most difficult.

f At first I was nervous.

No home. No job. No worries.

When he lost his flat, writer CJ Stone decided to 'go on the road'. How will he cope with life in the slow lane?

I didn't wake up one morning and say to myself, 'I think I'll go and live in a van.' It was more accidental than that. First of all I lost my flat and then, at the same time, I discovered I needed a new engine for my car. That meant that I would have to spend £1,000 to get the car back on the road. I suddenly found that I needed, first, somewhere to live and, second, something to travel around in.

[1] So I rang the number in the ad and arranged to go and see it. It was love at first sight! I made my decision straightaway. Two days later I was the proud owner of a two-litre Ford Transit converted into a camper van.

[2] I wasn't sure I could handle it. Where would I park? How would I wash? What would I do in the evenings? I'm the sort of person who needs people around, but you can't give big parties in a van. And how would I cope anyway with life on the road? But I needn't have worried. Well, not much. It's a lot easier than I thought.

[3] So far I've slept in several car parks and lay-bys, one or two festival sites and – once or twice – just by the roadside. I haven't yet found the perfect place. I spend a lot of time poring over maps for ideal sites. I ask around among the travellers. And I've no doubt I'll find a site. I'm an optimist – all my life I've always believed I have a place in the world.

[4] I suppose it's just the excitement of waking up in the morning, and, for the first few seconds, not knowing where you are. Then you look out of the window, and some new sight greets you: some tree you've never seen before, or some beautiful scenery that makes your heart leap. Living in a flat in the city I missed all that.

[5] After all, I'm a writer. To start with I stayed on campsites that had electricity whenever I wanted to work. But it cost money and I couldn't concentrate because everyone else was on holiday and playing games right outside my windows. And then I found the solution: solar panels. That meant I could stay anywhere. Now I'm not only a travelling writer, I'm ecologically sound too.

[6] Living in a van is cheap. No rent. No obligations. And on top of that there's the sense of freedom and the happiness that my new lifestyle has given me. Freedom can be addictive. I love being able to go where I want, when I want. It's wonderful to feel that the whole world is your home. No wonder so many people are leaving their houses and going on the road.

5 **Fact check** Answer the following questions.

a What is CJ Stone's job?
b Where does he live?
c What does he think of it?

6 **Read the text again and complete the following sentences.**

a CJ Stone decided to live as he does because …
b CJ Stone worried about his decision because …
c CJ Stone has parked in many places, such as …
d CJ Stone loves his new life because …
e CJ Stone solved his computer problems by …
f The advantages of living 'on the road' are …

7 **Vocabulary** What's the difference between:

a … an *accident* and something that is *accidental*?
b … a *park* and a *car park*?
c … a *site* and a *sight*?
d … a *road sign* and the *roadside*?
e … *poring over* and *pouring*?
f … a *campsite* and a *camper van*?

8 **Noticing language** Read the last four paragraphs of the text again. How many contractions (*I'm, he's, they've,* etc.) can you find? What does the use of contractions tell you about the style of the text?

Language in chunks

9 Explain the meaning of the following phrases from the text.

a a sense of freedom
b to cope with
c to have no doubt (that)
d to make a decision
e to spend a lot of time (doing something)

10 Complete the following sentences using the phrases in Activity 9. You may need to change the form of the verbs.

a I can't .... computers. I just don't understand them.

b He .... writing stories on his computer. He never seems to stop!

c I'm not sure whether to buy a camper van, but I'm going to .... soon.

d Walking in the countryside gives me ....

e He wants to marry her. He .... she's the one for him.

11 Discussion What is your reaction to CJ Stone's way of life? Would you do what he does? Why? Why not?

Grammar: the present perfect

12 Speaking In a circle, talk about things you've never done, but which you would like to do one day. Use the present perfect. Look at 5A–5C in the Mini-grammar. Remember to say what the previous students have said.

Example: BEN: I've never been to New York.

   SUE: Ben's never been to New York. I've never lived in a camper van.

   CAROL: Ben's never been to New York. Sue's never lived in a camper van. I've never ridden an elephant.

13 Complete the following sentences with the correct form of the verb in brackets and either *since* or *for*.

a Ashley (live) has lived in a camper van for three years.

b He (be) .... a writer .... October 1999.

c His wife, Stella, (work) .... on an organic farm .... Ashley gave up his job.

d They (not / eat) .... any meat .... two years.

e Ashley (speak) .... French .... he was a child.

f They (be) .... married .... ten years.

g I (not / see) .... them .... last January.

h He (have) .... a shaved head .... May last year.

Check your answers by looking at 5D in the Mini-grammar.

14 Just and yet Complete the dialogue with *just* (a short time ago) or *yet* (up until now).

JANE: Why are you so happy?

KATE: I've (**a**) .... heard that I've won a million pounds.

JANE: That's fantastic! What are you going to do with it?

KATE: I haven't decided (**b**) ....

JANE: But you must have dreamed of this moment.

KATE: Well yes, but it's only (**c**) .... happened. I'm still in shock.

JANE: Have you told your husband yet?

KATE: No. I've only (**d**) .... found out myself!

JANE: But you are going to, aren't you?

KATE: I haven't made a decision about that (**e**) ....

JANE: Hey, wait a minute! I've (**f**) .... had an idea. You could lend me some money!

KATE: Mmm …

Check your answers by looking at 5C in the Mini-grammar.

15 Present perfect and past simple Choose the past simple or present perfect forms for the verbs in brackets.

a I (live) in a houseboat for six years and I still do.
   I've lived in a houseboat for six years and I still do.

b I never (be) to Bangladesh.

c When I (leave) school two years ago, I (feel) a great sense of freedom.

d He (always / be) a pessimist, since the moment he (is) born.

e She couldn't cope with his behaviour so she (leave) him. That (be) two years ago.

f I (never / live) in a block of flats, but my parents (live) in a flat when they (be) first married.

g She (have) a tattoo for six months. She (go) to a place in town to get it done.

h When I (be) younger, my grandparents (speak) Russian so I (pick) up a few words, but I can't speak it properly.

16 Copy the table (but not the handwriting). Think of four questions you'd like to ask people about their life experiences. Write them in your table.

Go round the class asking your questions. When someone says '*yes*', ask them for details.

Have you ever …	*broken a leg?*
Name	*Kim*
Details	*5 years ago, fell off a horse*

Example:

STUDENT A: *Have you ever broken a leg, Pablo?*

STUDENT B: *No.*

STUDENT A: *Have you ever broken a leg, Kim?*

STUDENT C: *Yes.*

STUDENT A: *When did you break it?*

STUDENT C: *About five years ago.*

STUDENT A: *How did you do it?*

STUDENT C: *I was riding my horse one morning and I fell off. It was very painful.*

Vocabulary: homes and houses

17 Match the words in the box with the numbers in the pictures.

> basement   block of flats   bungalow   cottage   fence   flat
> first floor   garage   garden   gate   ground floor
> semi-detached house   terraced house   studio flat

Example: 1 *block of flats*

18 Discussion Which of the pictures is most like where you live? What differences are there between your home and the one in the picture?

Using a dictionary: definitions and examples

19 Look at the dictionary entry for *garden* and answer the following questions.

a Is *garden* an adjective, adverb, noun, preposition or verb? How do you know?
b How is it pronounced?
c What equivalent word is there in American English?
d How many different meanings are given?

gar·den¹ S1 W1 /ˈgɑːdn $ ˈgɑːr-/ n
1 [C] *BrE* the area of land next to a house, where there are flowers, grass, and other plants, and often a place for people to sit; ⊟ **yard** *AmE: He's outside in the garden.* | *Grace brought us some flowers from her garden.* | *Our house has a small garden.* | *a garden shed* | **back/front garden** (=at the back or the front of the house)
2 [C] *AmE* a part of the area next to a house, which has plants and flowers in it: **vegetable/herb/rose garden** *The house has a beautiful herb garden.*
3 gardens [plural] a large area of land where plants and flowers are grown so that the public can go and see them: *the Botanical Gardens at Kew*
4 Gardens *BrE* used in the name of streets: *211 Roland Gardens* → KITCHEN GARDEN, MARKET GARDEN; → **lead sb up the garden path** at LEAD¹ (12)

20 Practice Which of the homes above would you like to live in? Which would you not like to live in? Why?

Examples: I'd like to live in the cottage because it's very pretty.

I wouldn't like to live in the block of flats because the rooms are very small.

21 Make new words by adding *home* to the following words. Use the new words in the newspaper headlines below.

___sick   ___coming   ___less   ___-grown   ___work   ___-made

a ....Home-grown. lettuce sells best
b .... man wins lottery, buys house
c .... cake poisons entire village
d .... couple return after only 72 hours away
e .... crisis in our schools
f .... celebration cancelled when returning son misses transatlantic flight

Listening: Making myself homeless

22 Think about your home. Write five adjectives to describe:

a ... what it looks like.
b ... what it feels like.

23 Match the phrases on the left with their meanings on the right.

a a sense of freedom   someone who thinks everything will be terrible

b a camper van   a feeling that you are free

c to hit the road   a van that you can sleep in

d Home is where the heart is.   to feel as if you do not have any friends

e to be homeless   to not have a home

f to be lonely   someone who thinks everything will be wonderful

g an optimist   anywhere that you feel comfortable is home

h a pessimist   to go travelling

24 You are going to hear a song called *Making myself homeless*. Here are the first and the last verses. What order should the lines go in? Write the numbers in the brackets.

First verse:
a [ ] I don't feel like staying in.
b [ ] I'm sitting here without you
c [ ] It's cold and it's empty
d [ ] The light is getting dim

Last verse:
e [ ] And my travelling days will be done
f [ ] And we'll have our new day in the sun.
g [ ] And we'll go back home one fine morning
h [ ] And you'll come running towards me

Listen to the song on Track 25. Did you get the first and the last verses right?

25 Which of these summaries (*a–c*) best describes the song?

a The singer is unhappy because his camper van is cold and empty, and it is raining. He wants to travel to the road's end.

b The singer is unhappy because his girlfriend has left him. He leaves home and travels in a camper van. He hopes he will meet his girlfriend again and that they will go back home together.

c The singer is unhappy because his house is cold and empty so he decides to go on the road. It rains a lot, but he's looking forward to a day when it will be sunny again.

26 Complete these lines from the song.

a So I guess I'll ....

b I'm not a .... or an ....

c I just need to have ....

d And the light is .... at the road's ....

e And I'll forget about you if ....

f And the road stretches ....

g I can do whatever ....

h For what use is travelling ....

i It just makes me homesick for ....

j But the road leads ....

27 Listen to Track 25 again and follow the lyrics in the Audioscript. Complete this sentence:

I like / don't like the song because

....

....

Functional language: welcoming people

28 Look at the picture. What are they saying to each other?

Listen to Track 26. Were you correct?

29 Match the phrases in the two columns to complete the welcoming sentences.

Can I get you	finding us?
Can I take	into the sitting room.
Did you have any trouble	something to drink?
Do you want / need	to see you!
Go on	to wash your hands / freshen up?
How nice	for coming.
Thanks	your coat?

Listen to Track 27 and repeat the phrases.

30 Put the phrases from Activity 29 in the correct gaps.

a '*Can I get you something to drink?*' 'Yes please. I'd like an orange juice.'

b '...' 'No. It was quite straightforward, actually.'

c '...' 'Thank you.'

d '...' 'Thank you. Is it through here?'

e '...' 'Yes, that would be nice. Where's the bathroom?'

f '...' 'Well, thanks for inviting us.'

g '...' 'Yes. It's great to be here.'

●●● Pronunciation: stress in phrases

31 Look at the replies in Activity 30. Listen to Track 28 and write a line under the word or the part of the word where the speakers place the main stress.

I'd like an orange juice.

32 Repeat the phrases after the speakers on Track 28.

33 Role-play Work in groups. One of you is the host. You have invited people round for a drink. Welcome them to your house / flat using the phrases from Activity 29. The rest of you are the guests. Respond to your host using phrases from Activity 30.

Writing: letters

34 Study the letter and make notes about the following questions.

a Where is Brenda writing from?
b How did she and Mariel get there?
c How did she feel when she first arrived? How does she feel now?
d What differences are there between Brenda's and Mariel's characters?
e What is Brenda's job? What is Mariel's?
f Who is David?
g How formal is the letter? How do you know?

35 Would you use the following in letters which are *Formal* (F) or *Informal* (I) or *Neutral* (neither formal nor informal) (N)?

a Hi Rosemary
b Dear Mrs Forrest
c Dear James
d Dear Ms Forrest
e Dear Sir or Madam
f With best wishes
g Lots of love
h Yours sincerely
i Yours faithfully
j Love
k Thanks for your letter.
l Thank you very much for your letter.
m Please give my love to David and the kids.
n I look forward to hearing from you.

36 You are going to write a letter. Make notes on the following.

a Choose somewhere in the world you like the sound of. Imagine that you are now living there.
b How did you get there?
c What kind of job do you normally do? Have you found something similar in your new place?
d Where are you living in your new country? What kind of a place is it?
e What English-speaking friend or relative (real or imaginary) could you write to?

Using your notes, write a letter to your English-speaking friend or relative. Use the language from Brenda's letter to help you.

Flat 3
156 Centenary Road
Mumbai
India

15th June

Dear Rosemary,

I've just received your letter – thanks. It was nice to hear from you.

Well, we've been here for three weeks already. I still can't believe it. But things have definitely improved since the bus left us at the roadside on that first day. For a minute I wanted to turn round and go home again. You know me, I'm a great pessimist. But Mariel always thinks everything is going to be fine. In less than a day she had found us a flat and here we are.

I've found myself a job giving private conversation classes. Not quite what I'm used to, but it's still teaching and my students are lovely. Mariel hasn't got a job yet, but she's made contact with various people in the film industry here and hopes she'll get work soon.

So the big news is, we've made our decision. We've decided to stay. This is our home.

Please give my love to David and the kids. Why not come and visit us soon?

Lots of love,
Brenda

Review: grammar and functional language

37 Complete the conversation with the correct present perfect or past simple form of the verb in brackets.

ALAN: How nice to see you!

BARBARA: It's nice to be here.

CLARE: (**a** you / have) .... any trouble finding us?

DAN: Oh no. We (**b** be) .... here before, you know.

ALAN: Oh, really? But we (**c** only / live) .... here for three weeks.

BARBARA: Yes. But we knew the people who (**d** live) .... here before you.

CLARE: You mean Sara and Jeff?

DAN: Yes. They (**e** be) .... friends of ours since we met them at university.

ALAN: How interesting. Well, anyway, can I take your coats?

BARBARA: Thanks.

CLARE: Go on through to the sitting room. I expect you know your way!

38 Complete the following sentences if they apply to you.

I live in ....

I study English at ....

I have pierced ears / a tattoo / a beard / a moustache.

I wear glasses / contact lenses / lots of jewellery.

I play / do (sport, musical instrument, hobby).

I work in / at / as ....

I am engaged / married / single.

Give your sentences to your partner.

39 Interview your partner about the sentences in front of you.
Ask *How long ...* ?

Example: *How long have you lived in London Road?*

Write a short paragraph about your partner's answers using *since* and *for*.

Review: vocabulary

accident   accidental   bare   basement   block of flats   bungalow
campsite   camper van   car park   cluttered   cold   cottage
cramped   dark   fence   first floor   flat   garage   garden   gate
guest   ground floor   homecoming   homeless   home-made
homesick   homework   host   houseboat   light   mobile home
optimist   park   pessimist   road sign   roadside   semi-detached
house   sight   spacious   studio flat   tent   terraced house   tidy
untidy   warm

a sense of freedom
to cope with
to go on the road
to have no doubt (that)
to make a decision
to spend a lot of time
  (doing something)

40 Think about which six words in the Word List will be most useful to you in the future. Why?

41 Copy and complete the tables with words from the Word List.

Words with a positive feeling	Words with a negative feeling

Pronunciation

42 a What sound do all the following words have in common?

bungalow   cold   cope   go   homeless   mobile home   studio

Listen to Track 29 and check.

b Can you find other words in the Word List which include the same sound?

Listen to Track 30 and check.

c Which words in the Word List start with the following sounds:
/bl/:
/kr/:
/gr/:
/sp/:

Listen to Track 31 and check.

d Which sound do you find the most difficult to say?

e List some other words that start with these sounds:
/bl/:
/kr/:
/gr/:
/sp/:

43 Using as many words as possible from the Word List, expand the following sentence. Who can make the longest sentence which still makes sense?

The woman left the next day.

44 Writing In groups of five, you are going to write a poem called *On the road*.

a Each take a different phrase from Word Plus.
b Each use the phrase to write a short sentence about life on the road.
c As a group, arrange the sentences in the best way you can to make your poem.

Vocabulary: different histories

1   Complete the sentences in each box using the words in the column on the left.

IN A COURT OF LAW

guilty
prison
sentence
accuse

a I .... you of stealing £250,000.

b We think he is ....

c I .... you to ten years in ....

HIGH ADVENTURE

disguised
escaped
pirate
soldiers
captured

d Mad John, the ...., was .... by the king's ....

e They put him in prison, but he ...., ... as a woman.

WAR AND PEACE

defeated
crowned
elected
conquered

f When he .... the country, he .... himself king.

g Ten years later the king was .... in battle.

h The people .... a president instead.

died

executed

poison

shot

stabbed

i The first Lord Mountebank .... when he drank ....

j Ten years later someone .... his son with a knife.

k The third Lord Mountebank was ....

l The fourth was .... by a jealous lover.

---

born

brought up

divorced

educated

inherited

married

m She was .... in 1923. She was .... by her uncle.

n She was .... at the best school in America.

o She .... $35 million when her uncle died.

p She was .... three times – and got .... three times too.

2 Copy and complete the table with the following verbs.

| accuse | bring up | conquer | crown | defeat | die | disguise | divorce | educate | elect |
| escape | execute | imprison | inherit | marry | poison | sentence | shoot | stab |

a Verb (infinitive)	b Verb (past participle)	c Noun
accuse	accused	accusation

3 Play the 'teapot game'. Write sentences using the word *teapot* instead of one of the words from Activities 1 and 2. The other students have to guess the word.

Examples:

STUDENT A: I'd like to be a teapot because then I could fight for my country.

STUDENT B: Soldier?

STUDENT A: Yes.

STUDENT A: You can kill someone by giving them some teapot.

STUDENT C: Poison?

STUDENT A: Yes.

Using a dictionary: same word, different meanings

4 Look at the dictionary entry for *crown*.

a How many different meanings are given for the noun?

b If 'S3' means that *crown* is one of the 3,000 most common words in spoken English, what does 'W3' mean?

c What does '[C]' mean? Is that the same as 'usually singular'?

crown¹ S3 W3 /kraʊn/ n
1 HAT FOR KING/QUEEN [C] **a)** a circle made of gold and decorated with jewels, worn by kings and queens on their heads **b)** a circle, sometimes made of things such as leaves or flowers, worn by someone who has won a special honour
2 COUNTRY'S RULER the crown **a)** the position of being king or queen: *The treaty of Troyes made Henry V heir to the crown of France.* **b)** the government of a country such as Britain that is officially led by a king or queen: *He has retired from the service of the Crown.*
3 TOOTH [C] an artificial top for a damaged tooth
4 HEAD [usually singular] the top part of a hat or someone's head: [+of] *auburn hair piled high on the crown of her head* | *a hat with a high crown*
5 HILL [usually singular] the top of a hill or something shaped like a hill: [+of] *They drove to the crown of Zion hill and on into town.* | *The masonry at the crown of the arch is paler than on either curve.*
6 SPORTS [usually singular] the position you have if you have won an important sports competition: *Can she retain her Wimbledon crown?* | *He went on to win the world crown in 2001.*
7 MONEY [C] **a)** the standard unit of money in some European countries: *Swedish crowns* **b)** an old British coin. Four crowns made a pound.
8 PICTURE [C] a mark, sign, BADGE etc in the shape of a crown, used especially to show rank or quality

C

Reading: three lives

5 Read about one of these three women. Copy and complete the table on page 59 about her.

FAMOUS WOMEN

Mary Read, one of the most famous female pirates in history, was born in London in 1690. Her father died when she was young and Mary's mother raised her as a boy. Only male children could inherit money so Mary was disguised as a boy so that she would inherit her grandmother's money.

When Mary was 13 she joined a ship, still dressed as a man. A few years later she joined the British army (as a man) and was sent to fight the French in Holland. There she fell in love with one of her fellow soldiers — and had to reveal her secret, much to everyone's surprise!

When her husband died, Mary put on men's clothes again and joined a ship going to the West Indies. But the ship was captured by English pirates, led by Jack Rackham and Anne Bonney. Mary decided to become a member of the pirate crew. She fell in love again, this time with a soldier they had captured, and was married. But their honeymoon was short because Mary and her fellow pirates, Jack and Anne, were taken prisoner near Jamaica and were sentenced to death. Mary was saved from death because she was pregnant, but she died in prison in 1720.

Calamity Jane was a heroine of the American Wild West, famous for her bravery. A film was made about her in 1953, starring Doris Day.

Calamity Jane's real name was Martha Jane Cannary and she was born in 1852 in Missouri, USA. Her parents were farmers. As a young girl she could ride a horse and shoot a gun as well as any man. In the 1870s, dressed as a man, she fought with the army against the Native Americans. During a fierce battle, the captain was shot and fell from his horse. She lifted him on to her own horse and saved him. When he recovered, the captain said, 'I name you Calamity Jane, the heroine of the plains.'

In 1876 Calamity Jane met Wild Bill Hickock and they settled in the town of Deadwood, Dakota. The same year, Wild Bill was shot in the back of the head while playing cards in a saloon bar.

Calamity Jane left Deadwood. For a time she raised cattle and kept an inn. Then she moved to California, and later to El Paso, Texas, where she married Clinton Burke. They had a daughter, but the marriage was not a success. Calamity Jane never had much money and died a poor woman in 1903. She was buried in Deadwood next to Wild Bill Hickock, as she had requested.

Cristina Sánchez was one of the only female bullfighters, or 'matadors', of modern times. She was forced to stop fighting bulls because of criticism — many people thought that bullfighting was only for men.

Women in Spain have fought bulls since the 18th century, but a law in 1908 banned them on the grounds of 'decency and public morality'. The ban was lifted briefly in the 1930s when Spain became a republic, but was put back again by the dictator Francisco Franco. The ban was lifted again after Franco's death in 1976 — but even then most women only fought on horseback. Cristina fought on foot.

Cristina was born in Madrid, Spain, in 1972. She started her bullfighting career in South America when she was only 20. She attracted a lot of attention and soon became a matador back in Spain. However, Cristina was frequently criticised by male bullfighters.

A lot of people believed that women in the ring were unlucky. 'Women should be in the kitchen, backing up men. It's unnatural for them to fight,' said Jesulin de Ubrique, a typical critic. Many male bullfighters refused to appear with her.

Cristina Sánchez retired in 1999 because she was fed up with the attitude of the other matadors and some of the public. But, almost certainly, she won't be the last female matador.

Name		
a Dates (birth / death):	**d** Main events in her life:	
b Nationality:	**e** Important people in her life:	
c What was special about her:	**f** How/why her career ended:	

6 Find two members of the class who read about the other women. Interview them and complete your table with the information they give you.

Example: STUDENT A: *When was Mary Read born?*

STUDENT B: *She was born in 1690.*

Language in chunks

7 Complete the sentences with the phrases from the box. (You might have to change the tense of some verbs.)

much to my surprise   on foot   on horseback   the ban was lifted   fall in love with   settle in

a My great-grandfather was a village carpenter. His family was very poor. As a boy he had to go to school ....

b He .... my great-grandmother when he saw her at a dance.

c My great-grandfather wanted to live in the capital city, but in those days you were not allowed to move away from your own village. However, ... just after my great-grandparents got married.

d In the end they .... the capital city. They rode there ....

e I wrote an essay about my great-grandfather for a competition at school. .... I won first prize for it.

8 Use the phrases from Activity 7 to retell the following story.

Kristina the Tuneful was a musician. She went to live in Kleff when music was permitted again after the rule of Bad Queen Margaret. One day, riding her horse, she went to the neighbouring village of Steiv and saw Stanislav the Carpenter. He was incredibly handsome. It was love at first sight! She thought he could never feel the same about her, but he did!

9 Who was:

a ... captured by English pirates?
b ... criticised by male bullfighters?
c ... known for her bravery?
d ... disguised as a boy?
e ... buried next to Wild Bill Hickock?
f ... shot in a saloon bar?
g ... forced to end her career because of criticism?
h ... sentenced to death but was saved?

10 Noticing grammar What do you notice about the verbs in the questions in Activity 9?

11 Discussion Which of the three women do you find most interesting? Why?

Grammar: the passive

12 Read the following information about the Great Pyramid and underline the passive verbs. Use **6A in the Mini-grammar** to help you.

The Great Pyramid was built in Egypt about 5,000 years ago. It was constructed to the west of the River Nile. This area was called 'The Land of the Dead'. The Great Pyramid was made from huge blocks of limestone. The wheel had not yet been invented, so the blocks of stone were pulled from the quarry by hundreds of men on a path of wooden logs. The pyramid was designed with a solid core of limestone with four sides, and gaps were left for corridors and various rooms. It is not known exactly what the pyramids were used for, but burial chambers (where the bodies of dead pharaohs and their families and servants were placed) have been found deep inside the pyramids. It is thought that pyramids were designed to help the pharaoh's spirit rise up to the sun after death. The pyramids are visited by millions of people each year.

13 Now read the following information about the famous ship the *Titanic* and write the correct passive form of the verb in brackets in each gap.

The *Titanic* (**a** build) .... in 1912. It (**b** design) .... in a new way and it was (**c** think) .... to be unsinkable. Because of this, it (**d** not/give) .... enough lifeboats for the passenger and crew. The hull (**e** damage) .... by a collision with a huge iceberg and it sank very fast. A total of 1,513 people (**f** drown) .... that day. Because of this disaster, new

international safety laws (**g** pass) .... and the Ice Patrol (**h** establish) .... In 1985 the wreck (**i** locate) .... on the sea bed and the ship (**j** explore) .... Several successful films (**k** make) .... about the Titanic since then, and the most recent (**l** release) .... in 1997.

14 Read **6D in the Mini-grammar** and then make two passive sentences from each of the following statements. The beginning of the first two sentences is given.

a The chef baked a huge cake for the president's daughter.
  A huge cake ...
  The president's daughter ...

b The director of the gallery showed the journalists the new sculpture.

c A record company offered Robbie Williams a multi-million dollar contract recently.

d The government granted some war veterans a pardon.

e The academy awarded Nadia Kastelitz the state literature prize.

f The committee gave Viktor Selianov a gold medal for bravery.

15 Choose a famous person from the following list or think of your own. Make passive sentences about them. Use the words from Activity 1 on pages 55–56 to help you.

> Mao Tse-tung   Robin Hood   Simon Bolivar
> Marie Antoinette   Snow White   Julius Caesar
> Cinderella   Princess Diana   Garibaldi
> John Lennon   Nelson Mandela

Example: One of the most famous people in English history is Oliver Cromwell. He led the Civil War against King Charles I. After Charles was executed, Cromwell was made Lord Protector in 1653. He was offered the crown in 1657, but he refused it.

Listening: a 'whodunnit'

16 Listen to Track 32. Who is:

a ... Arthur Logan?
b ... Joshua Logan?
c ... Juliet Logan?
d ... Crawford Jarvis?

17 **Fact check** Listen to Track 32 again. Who:

a ... was murdered?
b ... was hit on the back of the head (but not murdered)?
c ... couldn't get to sleep?
d ... went for a walk in the garden?

18 On Track 32 who says:

a 'He's been in love with my aunt for years.'
b 'I can't bear to think about it.'
c 'I didn't kill Joshua Logan, honestly.'
d 'I have a lot on my mind.'
e 'I was woken by a sound downstairs.'
f 'It's no secret.'
g 'It's not true.'
h 'You and your husband haven't been getting on well.'
i 'Some people in your situation might think of killing their husband.'

19 Who do you think killed Joshua Logan?

20 Listen to Track 33. Does Inspector Wade agree with you? How did she know who killed Joshua Logan?

21 **Noticing grammar** Look at Track 32 in the Audioscript. How many examples of the passive can you find?

22 There are many books and television programmes about detectives who solve murder mysteries. Which are the most popular in your country? Which do you like the best?

Functional language: paying compliments

23 Before you listen to Track 34, put these lines in the correct conversations.

> I was given them by my aunt.   From that shop opposite the bank.   It was a present from my girlfriend.

HELEN: That's a really nice jacket.
SAM: Oh, thanks.
HELEN: Where did you get it?
SAM: (a) ....
HELEN: Oh yes. I know the one. Well, it really suits you.
SAM: Thanks.

JASON: I like your shirt.
LEO: Do you?
JASON: Yes.
LEO: (b) ....
JASON: Well, it looks good on you. What's it made of?
LEO: I don't know. Cotton, I think.

SUNITA: Those are really nice earrings.
KAREN: I'm glad you like them.
SUNITA: Where did you get them?
KAREN: (c) ....
They're from Japan, I think.
SUNITA: Well, I think they're great.

Now listen to Track 34. Were you correct?

24 Complete the table with language from the conversations in Activity 23 on the previous page.

Saying you like something:	That's a really nice jacket.
Saying something is good for the person who is wearing it:	
Being pleased that someone compliments you:	

25 Vocabulary Do you know these words?

> corduroy   cotton   denim   leather   nylon
> plastic   polyester   silk   wool

Choose six words from the list to match the things in the picture.

26 Ask about things people in the class are wearing.

Example: STUDENT A: What are your shoes made of?

STUDENT B: I don't know. Leather, I think.

27 Role-play Work in pairs. Have conversations in which one of you compliments the other on something they are wearing.

Speaking: interviewing a portrait

◐ ◑ ● Pronunciation: showing interest

28 Listen to the man's responses on Track 35. Write a line under the main stress in the following phrases.

  a That's fant<u>a</u>stic.
  b How inter<u>e</u>sting!
  c That is int<u>e</u>resting.
  d Oh, really?
  e You're thinking of getting married?
  f You live in Birmingham?

29 Say the sentences like the speaker on Track 35.

30 Creative task You are going to interview one of the people pictured here.

a Work in groups. Choose one of the people in the pictures. Write as many questions for them as you can. You can ask about who they are, how they are feeling, what they have for breakfast, what their favourite music is, etc.

b One student plays the part of the person you have chosen. That student should look at the person, trying to imagine who they are, what their character is like, what kind of life they have, etc.

c Using the questions you have prepared, the other students interview the person. Show interest in the answers you are given by using the phrases in Activity 28.

Rachel

John Evelyn

Mr and Mrs Andrews

Writing: mini-biography

31 Imagine you are going to interview someone. Write questions in English to find out the following biographical information.

a Name
b Date and place of birth
c Background (nationality, where they have lived, education)
d Important events in their life
e Most recent important event
f How they would describe themselves
g Interests
h Future important events or hopes

32 Use your questions to interview someone who speaks English. Copy and complete the table.

a Name:

b Date and place of birth:

c Background (nationality, where they have lived, education):

d Important events in their life:

e Most recent important event:

f How they would describe themselves:

g Interests:

h Future important events or hopes:

33 Use your notes to write three short paragraphs about the person you interviewed. You can follow this plan.

Introduce the person, their background, and early events.

⬇

Describe the person and their interests.

⬇

Talk about the most recent events in their life and discuss what the future holds for them.

34 Look at the two pictures. Using words in the box say what has changed from the old room on the left to the new one on the right.

> a plant   blinds   the armchairs and sofa   the carpet   the lampshade
> the ornaments   the picture   a rug   the telephone   the walls

Example: *A plant has been put in the fireplace.*

BEFORE

AFTER

35 **Quiz** In teams, list some titles you know of things in Box A. Try to think of two examples for each.

Example: *books: 'One Hundred Years of Solitude' and 'The Beach'*

A	B
books buildings designs discoveries films inventions pieces of music plays poems works of art	build compose design direct discover invent paint write

Tell the other team one of the titles from your list. Using the verbs in Box B, they have to say who created that thing. Score one point for each correct answer.

Example: TEAM A: *'One Hundred Years of Solitude'.*

TEAM B: *It was written by Gabriel García Márquez.*

36 **Speaking** Think of a book, play, film or piece of music that you know well. Who wrote it, directed it, etc? Tell the story.

37 **Writing** Write a conversation between two people in which one person compliments the other on their clothing, their new furniture, their new car / bicycle, their watch, their mobile phone, etc.

Review: vocabulary

Word List

accuse	be born	bring up	bullfighter	capture		conquer
corduroy	cotton	crown	defeat	denim	die	disguise
divorced	educate	elect	escape	execute	guilty	
imprison	inherit	leather	marry	nylon	pirate	plastic
poison	polyester	prison	sentence (v)	shoot	silk	
soldier	stab	wool				

Word Plus

much to my surprise
on foot / horseback
to impose / lift a ban
to fall in love with
to settle in (name of a place)

38 Decide which words in the Word List have (a) a positive feeling,
(b) a negative feeling, or (c) a neutral feeling.

Pronunciation: syllables and stresses

39 a Find all the words from the Word List with two or more syllables. Which syllable is most often stressed: the first one, the last one, or the one before the last one?

Listen to Track 36 and check.

b Copy and complete the table with words from the Word List which include the letter 'o'. How is it pronounced in each case? Which 'o' word in the Word List doesn't fit in any of the boxes? Practise saying the words.

/ɔː/ - worn	/ɒ/ - song	/ɔɪ/ - boy	/ə/ - photograph	/əʊ/- oh!	/uː/- pool

Listen to Track 37 and check

40 Look at the Word List.

a Which words can be both nouns and verbs?
b Which words can be both nouns and adjectives? What word group do these words belong to?

41 Writing Continue the following fairy story using as many words and phrases from the Word List and Word Plus as possible. Who can use the most words?

Once upon a time there was a bad prince who fell in love with his beautiful young neighbour ...

Good intentions

→ future forms
→ phrasal verbs
→ promises and agreements

Grammar: the future

1 **Discussion** Read the following information about New Year. Is it the same as New Year in your country?

NEW YEAR'S EVE is December 31st. Many people go to parties or stay up and watch the New Year celebrations on television. It is common for people to make New Year's resolutions – promises to behave better in the following year (e.g. to stop eating so much chocolate, to take up exercise, etc). New Year's Day is January 1st. It is always a public holiday. Most people stay at home, recovering from the evening before.

2 Look at the picture and complete the speech bubbles with the following phrases.

answer the telephone	feel terrible
be the New Year	flying back to Australia
coming to lunch	leave my job
do more of the housework	got an interview
eat another chocolate bar	

Listen to Track 38. Were you correct?

3 Which of the sentences in Activity 2 are New Year's resolutions? Which are not?

4 Look at **7A–7E in the Mini-grammar**. Which of the grammar patterns were used in Activity 2?

● ● ● Pronunciation: how sounds change in contractions

5 Listen to the following sentences on Track 39. Does the sound of 'I' (/aɪ/) change in the examples? Why?

I will do it tomorrow. / I'll do it tomorrow.
I will have that coffee now, please. / I'll have that coffee now, please.
I will answer the telephone. / I'll answer the telephone.
I will talk to you later. / I'll talk to you later.
I will be home at nine. / I'll be home at nine.
I will never forget this. / I'll never forget this.

6 Say the contracted sentences in the same way as the speakers on Track 39.

'I'm going to (c) .... in the New Year. Honest!'

'If you go like that yo (f) .... tomorrow morning'

'Listen everybody! It'll (g) .... in exactly ten seconds!'

'From tomorrow I'm never going to (a) .... !'

'I'm going to (d) .... in the New Year. I've (e) .... on January 7th.'

'Who's (h) .... tomorrow, Margie?'

'I'm (b) .... in a week. I'm really looking forward to it.'

'Will somebody please (i) .... ?'

7 Look at 7A–7E in the Mini-grammar. Which future form would you choose in the following cases? (Often more than one is possible.)

a We (travel) to Boston on Sunday.
b He (go) to Manchester in May.
c I bet she (pass) her exam.
d I can't come to your party. I (play) in a concert that evening.
e I (never / forget) you, I promise.
f I (try) harder at school from now on.
g The train (arrive) at five-fifteen.
h Look! There's George. I need to speak to him. I (see) you in a minute.
i Oh no! Look at the fuel gauge. We (run out of) petrol.
j She (learn) how to windsurf on holiday next year.

8 Read the following sentences and choose which is better in the second sentence or phrase.

a The newspaper says it's going to snow.
It's probably going to snow. / ~~It's probably snowing.~~
b I have an appointment at the hairdresser tomorrow at 3.
I'm going to the hairdresser tomorrow. / I go to the hairdresser tomorrow.
c Mark is feeling very dizzy.
He faints. / He's going to faint.
d If the sail hits the water …
the boat will turn over. / the boat is turning over.
e I'm hungry. Come on, …
we have a sandwich. / let's have a sandwich.
f They've offered Penny a place at Bristol University!
The course is going to start in October. / The course starts in October.
g Yvonne and Frank are playing chess this afternoon.
Frank is definitely going to win. / Frank is definitely winning.
h I know!
I buy you a watch for your birthday! / I'll buy you a watch for your birthday!
i I can't quite reach that box of tissues on the top shelf.
Will you pass them to me, please? / Are you going to pass them to me, please?

Check your answers with **7A–7E in the Mini-grammar.**

9 Write notes about next weekend. Include:

a … two or three intentions.
b … two or three arrangements.
c … weather predictions.
d … two or three things you are definitely **not** going to do.

Now tell others about your expectations, plans and arrangements for the weekend.

Examples: It's probably going to rain.

I'm going to get up late on Sunday and do nothing! I'm not even going to think about work.

I'm meeting a friend at the cinema on Saturday evening.

Speaking: making arrangements

10 Work in groups of five.
STUDENT A: look at Activity Bank 10 on page 153.
STUDENT B: look at Activity Bank 16 on page 156.
STUDENT C: look at Activity Bank 18 on page 158.
STUDENT D: look at Activity Bank 21 on page 159.
STUDENT E: look at Activity Bank 23 on page 159.

11 Compare your decisions with other groups'.

Vocabulary: phrasal verbs

12 Work in pairs. Which of the following would you find most difficult to give up?

* chocolate
* shopping
* coffee
* watching TV
* going to clubs
* sugar
* listening to music
* something else: ....

13 Look at extracts from the dictionary entries for *give away*, *give back*, *give in to*, *give off*, *give out*.

give sb/sth **away** *phr v*
1 to give something to someone because you do not want or need it for yourself: *I gave most of my books away when I left college.* | [+to] *Give your old clothes away to a thrift shop.*
2 give somet ... to son ... ithout ask ... fo ... any

give off sth *phr v*
to produce a smell, light, heat, a sound etc: *The wood gave off a sweet, perfumed smell as it burned.* | *Try not to breathe in the fumes given off by the paint.*

give in to sth *phr v*
to no longer try to stop yourself from doing something you want to do: *Don't give in to the temptation to argue back.* | *If you feel the urge for a cigarette, try not to give in to it.*

man as part of a ...itional ...ng cere ...ony
give sth ⇔ **back** *phr v*
1 to give something to the person it belongs to or the person who gave it to you: *This isn't your money and you must give it back.* | *Of course you can have a look at it, as long as you give it back.* | **give sth back to sb** *I'll give the keys back to you tomorrow morning.* | **give sb** sth ⇔ **back** *Her ex-husband refused to give her back any of her old photos and letters.*
2 to make it possible for someo ... to h ... e or

give out *phr v*
1 give sth ⇔ out to give something to each person in a group; ⊟ **hand out**: *Can you give the drinks out, please?* | [+to] *Students were giving out leaflets to everyone on the street.*

Use the dictionary entries to answer these questions.

a Which of these phrasal verbs can be split up, with the object going between the verb (*give*) and the particle (*away*, *back*, *in to*, etc.)?
b Which of them cannot be split up?

14 Now look at the entry for *cut* in your dictionary, and answer these questions.

a How many phrasal verbs are made with this verb?
b Which of them (if any) can have the object between the verb and the particle?

15 Look at these resolutions that people made last New Year's Eve (December 31st). Replace the phrases in italics with one of the following phrasal verbs.

| break up with | cut down on | get round to | go on | make a go of | put in |
| see about | set up | take up | working out | | |

a 'I'm going to *make* my business *successful*.'

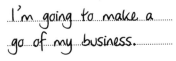
I'm going to make a go of my business.

b 'I'm going to *begin the hobby of* weight training.'

....

....

c 'We're going to *continue training* at the gym.'

(two phrasal verbs) ....

....

d 'We're going to *create* a new business.'

....

....

e 'I'm going to *finally start* building a new kitchen.'

....

....

f 'I'm going to *finish my relationship with* my girlfriend.'

....

....

g 'I'm going to *investigate the possibilities of* finding a job.'

....

....

h 'We're going to *reduce* the amount of wasted paper in the office.'...

....

i 'I'm going to *spend* more hours at the factory.'

....

....

16 Read the following description of the four different types of phrasal verb.

Different types of phrasal verb

Type 1 – The verb takes no object:
Flight 301 has already **taken off**.

Type 2 – The object can go after the phrasal verb or between the verb and the particle:
Can you **pick up** *Mr Smith?*
Can you **pick** *Mr Smith* **up**?
However, if the object is a pronoun (*me, you, him,* etc.) it can only go between the verb and particle:
Can you **pick** *him* **up**?
Not: ~~*Can you* **pick up** *him?*~~

Type 3 – The object always comes after the particle:
I'm not very good at **looking after** *children.*
Not: ~~*I'm not very good at* **looking** *children* **after**.~~

Type 4 – The phrasal verb has two or more particles, and the object always comes after the particles:
Oh no! We've **run out of** *petrol.*

What types are the phrasal verbs in Activity 15?

17 Choose any five of the phrasal verbs from Activities 12–15 and write a 'Find someone who …' questionnaire.

Find someone who:	Name
has given something up.	
has cut down on something recently.	
has never worked out in a gym.	

18 **Speaking** Now go round the class and complete your questionnaire with names. Find out as much information as you can.

Example: STUDENT A: Have you ever given anything up?

STUDENT B: No. Not yet!

STUDENT A: OK. Thanks. (Asks a different student.)
Have you ever given anything up?

STUDENT C: Yes. I gave up chocolate in January.

STUDENT A: Thanks. (Writes down C's name in their questionnaire.)

Tell the class anything interesting you have found out.

Reading: sticking to resolutions

19 Why do you think people find it difficult to stick to New Year's resolutions? What advice would you give someone about how to (a) stop doing something bad or (b) start doing something better?

20 Read the Internet text opposite by Dr Pauline Wallin. Do not use a dictionary unless you need to. Does she agree with your ideas on New Year's resolutions?

21 Read the text again and find:

a ... five resolutions that people sometimes make.
b ... three reasons why sticking to resolutions is difficult.

Which piece of advice do you think would be hardest to follow?

22 **Vocabulary** Explain the meaning of the following words from the text to another student.

a quit
b abandon
c visible
d challenge
e tips
f realistic
g goal
h drastically
i symptoms
j ingrained habits
k deprived

Make up sentences using the words.

Subjects

How to make those New Year's resolutions stick
by Dr Pauline Wallin

Every year on January 1 and 2, millions of us make New Year's resolutions. We'll say we are going to quit smoking or that we'll join a gym. We'll go on a diet or promise ourselves that from now on we're going to spend more time on housework or that we're going to cut down on all the chocolate we eat. But by February 2, most of these resolutions will be no more than a distant memory and we'll be behaving just the same as we were when the last year ended.

One reason why people abandon all their promises and resolutions is that it's easy to say we're going to do something (or not going to do something) but much harder to go on and on doing it (or not doing it) – especially if it is difficult or uncomfortable for us. OK, everyone may need a bit of a rest from all the eating and drinking over Christmas and the New Year, but a few weeks later our appetites have returned and we start to feel deprived. That's when we are most at risk – especially if the results of our dieting or not smoking are not immediately visible.

But don't despair! If you're thinking of making New Year's resolutions, first be sure you're ready for the challenge, and then read on for tips on how to increase your chances of success.

1 Examine your motivation for change. At the end of a long night, after a large meal, you say, 'That's it, I'm going on a diet tomorrow,' but the chances are you won't feel the same in 24 hours. However, if you are realistic and accept that change will be difficult, you will stay motivated for longer.

2 Set realistic goals. Habits and behaviours that are changed gradually have a greater chance of success than those that are changed so drastically that your mind and body just can't cope.

3 Focus on the programme rather than the goal. If you decide to control your eating, your goal for the day is not to lose a specific number of pounds, but to stick to your programme. Such focus on your behaviour will help you feel in control of your life. You will gain satisfaction from making sensible choices several times throughout the day.

4 Be positive about your physical symptoms. When you give up smoking you'll feel strange. See that as a good sign of your body getting rid of the drug, not as something unpleasant.

5 Stick to your decisions. Yesterday you said, 'I'm going to the gym at eight o'clock tomorrow morning.' But now it's quarter past seven in the morning and you don't feel like getting up. Tough! You'll never stick to those resolutions if you don't keep trying when it's difficult.

6 Nobody's perfect! You'll probably mess up from time to time. But you mustn't give in just because of that. Say to yourself, 'I'm going on with this – today, tomorrow and the next day. I'm not a quitter.'

7 If you're waiting for a more convenient time to begin to change your behaviour, that change won't happen. It's almost never convenient to change ingrained habits, so if you're going to do it, start right now. And then things will get better sooner!

Language in chunks

23 Complete the following sentences with these phrases from the text on page 71.

> on a diet   a distant memory   at risk   can't cope   in control of
>
> gain satisfaction   feel like   nobody's perfect

a 'What's the matter? You look worried.' 'I've got too much work just now. I just ....'

b 'Do you remember your tenth birthday clearly?' 'No, it's just ....'

c 'What's the matter?' 'I don't feel .... my life. Everything is going wrong.'

d 'I didn't do very well in my maths exam!' 'Oh, never mind, ...'

e 'Are you saying I'm overweight?' 'No! You don't need to go ....'

f 'Are you staying in tonight?' 'Yes, I don't .... going to Shelly's party.'

g 'You really think I can climb that mountain?' 'Yes I do, and you'll also

.... when you reach the top.'

h 'We've hardly sold any tickets for our show.' 'I know. It's .... of being cancelled.'

24 Play a conversation game. Write the phrases from the box in Activity 23 on separate pieces of paper. Place the papers face down in a pile.

In groups of three, choose one of the following subjects to discuss:

- Resolutions I haven't kept
- How life could be better
- The best way to celebrate (e.g. birthdays / New Year)

As the conversation develops, students pick up the pieces of paper in turn and use the phrase in the conversation. Who uses the phrases most successfully? The activity ends when all the pieces of paper have been used.

25 Noticing language Look at the text on page 71 again. How many different verb forms can you find which refer to the future? Which future verb form is used most? How many phrasal verbs can you find?

26 Role-play Work in pairs. One of you is having trouble sticking to a New Year's resolution. The other uses Dr Wallin's tips to help with the problem.

Example: STUDENT A: I can't go on like this. Not eating just makes me feel miserable and weak.

STUDENT B: You've got to be positive about your physical symptoms, not negative.

Functional language: making promises

27 Discussion Discuss the following questions about marriage in your country.

a Where do most people get married?

b What happens during the marriage ceremony?

c What words are used, and what do they mean in English?

28 Listen to Track 40 and match the extracts *1–4* with the pictures *a–d* below.

a ....

b ....

c ....

Are any of these like the kind of wedding you had or would like to have for yourself? Describe the kind of wedding that you had or hope for.

d ....

29 Listen to Track 40 again and complete the table with Ben's and Mariah's wedding vows.

	a I promise to:	b I agree to:	c I'll:	d I give you my word that:
Ben				
Mariah				

30 Writing Work in pairs. Write a conversation on one of the following themes using the language of promises and agreements.

a A couple are agreeing to get married. Like Ben and Mariah, they write their own wedding vows. What three things does he promise to do? What three things does she promise to do?

b A head teacher is talking to a pupil who has done something wrong. Decide what the pupil has done wrong and then think of what the head teacher asks him to do.

c Two flatmates are arguing about how to keep the flat tidy and who will do the cooking, etc. They decide to divide the housework (ironing, washing-up, cleaning, etc.). Who promises to do what?

d Two members of a pop group are discussing arrangements for a concert next weekend. What four things have to be done? Who promises / agrees to do which of them?

31 Look at the following words from a song and draw lines between the ones that rhyme.

ahead   day   down

late   right   said   song

straight   tonight   town

way   wrong

32 What do you think the song might be about? Make a note of your answer. Listen to Track 41 and check. Do you like the song?

33 Read these lines *a–i* from the song *No one's getting married any more*. Listen to the song on Track 41 so that you can put the letters *a*, *b*, *c*, etc. in the right order in the table below. Many letters will appear more than once.

a But when the lightning hits you, you just know then it's right
And that is why I'm sitting here to write these words tonight.

b I'll promise anything you want, I'll agree to what you say.
The only thing you have to do is turn up on some special day.

c I'm gonna add the sums up right to see what lies ahead,
The future's looking curious and nothing has been said.

d I'm gonna tell you something if I can get the words out straight,
But the trouble is I'm crazy and it's getting rather late.

e I've travelled long and hard, and I've been from town to town
And the thing I said I'd never do is try and settle down,

f No one's getting married anymore
So we could start a trend.
Or we could call it quits right now
And say we're just good friends. / 'This is the end.'

g Or maybe I'm an optimist and I've got the words all wrong,
Because first you write the melody and then you write the song.

h So I think I'll say it right out loud because I ain't got time to kill:
If you think it's getting serious and you want me to, I will.

i We're here at the departure gate, and I don't know what to say.
It seems to me we say 'goodbye', or we try some other way.

1	....
2	....
3	....
4	....
5	....
6	....
7	....
8	....
9	....
10	....
11	....
12	....
13	....

34 Discussion What does the singer really want?

35 Look at the following invitations *1–4* and answer the questions.

a Which is the most formal? Which is the most casual?

b Are the people who are sending the invitations young or old?

36 Read the invitations again and answer the questions.

a What information has to go on any invitation?

b What wording is used to invite the person in each case?

c What does the invitee have to do in each case? Is it always the same thing? What language is used for this?

d What do the following mean in an email?
  1 :-)
  2 CU
  3 BTW

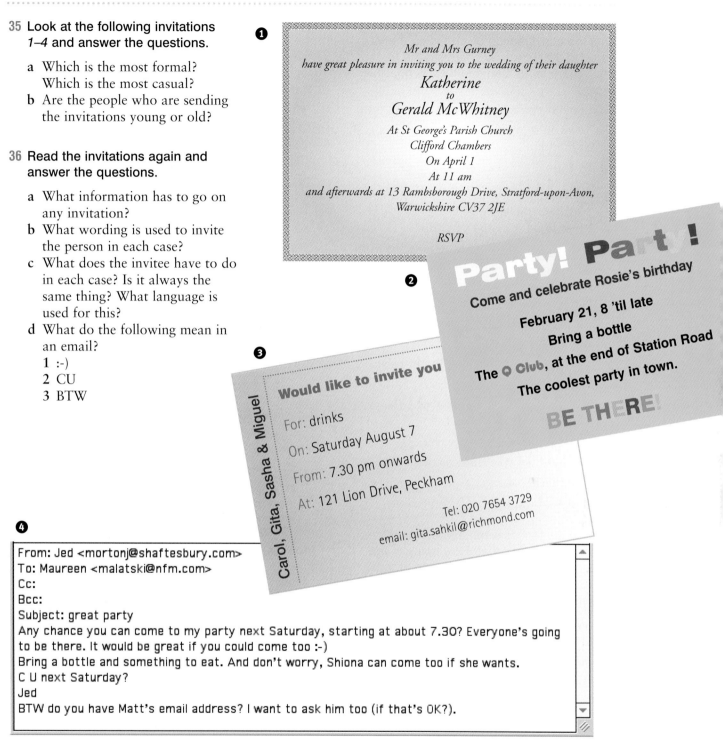

❶

Mr and Mrs Gurney
have great pleasure in inviting you to the wedding of their daughter
Katherine
to
Gerald McWhitney
At St George's Parish Church
Clifford Chambers
On April 1
At 11 am
and afterwards at 13 Rambsborough Drive, Stratford-upon-Avon,
Warwickshire CV37 2JE

RSVP

❷

Party! Party!
Come and celebrate Rosie's birthday
February 21, 8 'til late
Bring a bottle
The Q Club, at the end of Station Road
The coolest party in town.
BE THERE!

❸

Carol, Gita, Sasha & Miguel

Would like to invite you

For: drinks
On: Saturday August 7
From: 7.30 pm onwards
At: 121 Lion Drive, Peckham

Tel: 020 7654 3729
email: gita.sahkil@richmond.com

❹

From: Jed <mortonj@shaftesbury.com>
To: Maureen <malatski@nfm.com>
Cc:
Bcc:
Subject: great party
Any chance you can come to my party next Saturday, starting at about 7.30? Everyone's going to be there. It would be great if you could come too :-)
Bring a bottle and something to eat. And don't worry, Shiona can come too if she wants.
C U next Saturday?
Jed
BTW do you have Matt's email address? I want to ask him too (if that's OK?).

37 Creative task Imagine that you are planning a party to celebrate an event such as the end of a course, New Year's Eve, or an important birthday. You have unlimited money for your party.

a Work in groups. Decide:
  ... where the party should be.
  ... when it should start and end.
  ... what music there should be.
  ... what food and drink you want.
  ... what will make your party special – one that people will remember.

b Compare your decisions with another group's. Were your phrases the same?

c Write an invitation for the party you have decided to hold. Base it on one of the examples above.

38 Complete the conversation by choosing the most appropriate way of referring to the future, by changing the form of the verb in brackets. Where more than one form is possible, give reasons for your choice.

KAREN: Look at those black clouds. I think it (**a**) .... (rain).

GAIL: Yes, you're right. How (**b**) .... you .... (travel) to the city?

KAREN: By train.

GAIL: I (**c**) .... (drive) you to the station then.

KAREN: That's really nice of you.

GAIL: What (**d**) .... you .... (do) in the city?

KAREN: That (**e**) .... (depend) on how I get on.

GAIL: What do you mean?

KAREN: Well, if the meeting finishes quickly I (**f**) .... (have) lunch with Janet. We arranged it when I spoke to her on the phone yesterday.

GAIL: And if it doesn't?

KAREN: Then I (**g**) .... (come) straight back here, probably.

GAIL: What (**h**) .... you .... (say) at the meeting?

KAREN: I (**i**) .... (try) and explain why the project is behind schedule.

GAIL: (**j**) .... that .... (be) easy?

KAREN: No, but I (**k**) .... (do) the best I can.

GAIL: Good luck!

KAREN: Thanks. I think I (**l**) .... (need) it.

39 Complete the sentences with *I agree*, *I promise*, *I'll* or *I give you my word that*. How many of the sentences can start with more than one of these phrases?

a .... I'll go on a driving course.

b .... make a go of this business – just you wait and see.

c .... see about your problem tomorrow. I haven't got the time right now.

d .... to break off my relationship with him – if you want me to.

e .... to get round to painting the kitchen – when I have time.

f .... to do more housework next week.

g .... to cut down on my eating.

h .... I will never go to a football match again!

40 Choose one of the following occupations, but don't tell the others which you've chosen.

actor   bus driver   engineer   firefighter   footballer
musician   nurse   policeman   refuse collector
scientist   teacher   writer

Make a New Year's resolution as if you were that person. The others have to guess who you are.

Example: STUDENT A: *I'm going to drive more carefully in the future.*

STUDENT B: *Are you a bus driver?*

STUDENT A: *Yes.*

Review: vocabulary

Word List

abandon   agree to   break off
challenge   cut down on   deprived
drastically   get round to   give up
goal   go on   ingrained   make a go of
promise to   put in   quit   realistic
resolution   see about   set up
symptoms   take up   tip   visible
work out

Word Plus

Nobody's perfect
a distant memory
at risk
in control of
on a diet
to feel like (doing something)
to gain satisfaction

41 Choose one word or one phrase from the Word List which is important to you and think why you have chosen it.

Example: I choose 'look after', because I like caring for animals.

●● Pronunciation

42 Copy and complete the table with words from the Word list and Word Plus which have the following sounds.

day /eɪ/	**cow** /aʊ/	**so** /əʊ/

Listen to Track 42 and check.

Can you think of any other words to add to the table? Write them in the correct column.

43 Work in pairs. Explain the meaning of one of the words or phrases from the Word List or Word Plus. Your partner has to guess which one it is.

Example: STUDENT A: Something from the past that I have almost forgotten.

STUDENT B: A distant memory.

44 Read the following letter to 'Doctor Help' who answers letters in a popular newspaper. Decide what the writer is talking about and put that in the brackets.

Dear Doctor Help,

Two weeks ago I finally decided to give up ( ). I've meant to do it for some time because ( ) obviously isn't good for me.
For the first few days I didn't have a problem, but now it's getting worse and worse. I want ( ) all the time and everywhere I look, other people seem to be ( ), so I am always faced with temptation.
I am nervous I am going to start ( ) again but I don't want to. Can you help me please?

Yours,
'Frightened of temptation'

Write Doctor Help's reply.

UNIT 8
You can't do that here!

→ modal verbs (obligation, recommendation and permissio
→ anti-social behaviour
→ asking for permission

Listening: tango

1 Look at the following pictures. What do you think is happening in each one?

a

b

c

d

Put the pictures in the correct order to tell the story.

2 Listen to the story on Track 43. Were you right?

3 **Vocabulary** What do you understand by the following American English words and phrases from Track 43?

a sidewalk
b permit
c plates
d precinct
e ma'am

4 Listen to Track 43 again. Complete the gaps in these sentences from the track. Use one word for each gap.

a You .... here.   [ ]

b Are you telling us we .... for people?   [ ]

c We .... do.   [ ]

d Well, I'm sorry, ma'am, 'might' isn't ....   [ ]

e You .... a permit to do this kind of thing.   [ ]

f It's parked illegally, so you'd better .... about it.   [ ]

g Do you know .... the tango, officer?   [ ]

h Come on! You .... it.   [ ]

Who says which line? The police officer (*PO*), the male dancer (*MD*), or the female dancer (*FD*)?

●● ● Pronunciation:
different accents

5 Look at the following words. What do they mean? Now listen to the words said first by an American and then by a British speaker on Track 44. Is the pronunciation the *Same* (*S*) or *Different* (*D*)?

a	advertisement	[ ]	f interesting	[ ]
b	brochure	[ ]	g lieutenant	[ ]
c	cinema	[ ]	h officer	[ ]
d	controversy	[ ]	i opinion	[ ]
e	entertainer	[ ]	j simultaneous	[ ]

6 When the pronunciation is different, what is the main difference in each case?
Say the words using either American or British pronunciation.

7 Discussion Do you ever see street performers (musicians, dancers, etc.) in the street? Do you give them money? Do you like them?

Speaking: comparing opinions

8 Vocabulary Complete the following opinions with an appropriate verb from the box.

drive	drop	have	let	light	listen to	make
paint	put up	ride	smoke	use		

I don't think people should ...

a .... litter.

b spray-................................ the walls.

c .... posters everywhere.

d .... their dogs foul the footpath.

In my opinion people should not ...

e .... a lot of noise in a quiet area late at night.

f .... a walkman near other people.

g .... bicycles on the pavement.

h .... an over-sensitive car alarm.

People shouldn't be allowed to ...

i .... a smoky bonfire in the middle of the day.

j .... too fast in built-up areas.

k .... mobile phones on the train.

l .... in public places.

9 Look at the dictionary entries for *light*, *paint* and *shout*.
Do these verbs always take an object? How do you know?

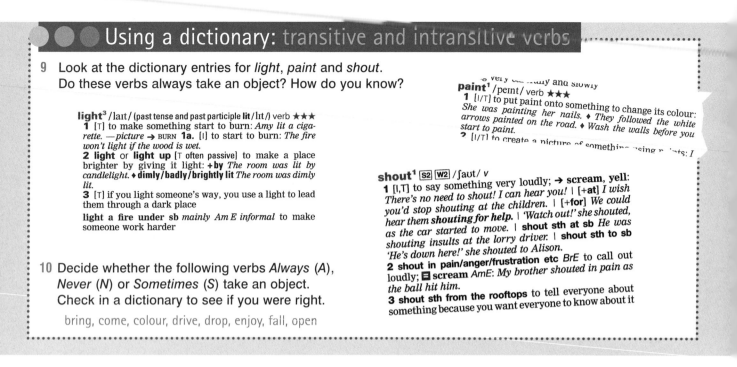

light³ /laɪt/ (past tense and past participle **lit** /lɪt/) verb ★★★
1 [T] to make something start to burn: *Amy lit a ciga-rette.* —*picture* → BURN **1a.** [I] to start to burn: *The fire won't light if the wood is wet.*
2 light or **light up** [T often passive] to make a place brighter by giving it light: **+by** *The room was lit by candlelight.* ♦ **dimly/badly/brightly lit** *The room was dimly lit.*
3 [T] if you light someone's way, you use a light to lead them through a dark place
light a fire under sb *mainly Am E informal* to make someone work harder

paint¹ /peɪnt/ verb ★★★
1 [I/T] to put paint onto something to change its colour: *She was painting her nails.* ♦ *They followed the white arrows painted on the road.* ♦ *Wash the walls before you start to paint.*
2 [I/T] to create a picture of something using paints: *I*

shout¹ S2 W2 /ʃaʊt/ v
1 [I,T] to say something very loudly; → **scream, yell:** *There's no need to shout! I can hear you!* | **[+at]** *I wish you'd stop shouting at the children.* | **[+for]** *We could hear them* **shouting for help.** | *'Watch out!' she shouted, as the car started to move.* | **shout sth at sb** *He was shouting insults at the lorry driver.* | **shout sth to sb** *'He's down here!' she shouted to Alison.*
2 shout in pain/anger/frustration etc *BrE* to call out loudly; ⊟ **scream** *AmE: My brother shouted in pain as the ball hit him.*
3 shout sth from the rooftops to tell everyone about something because you want everyone to know about it

10 Decide whether the following verbs *Always* (A),
Never (N) or *Sometimes* (S) take an object.
Check in a dictionary to see if you were right.

bring, come, colour, drive, drop, enjoy, fall, open

11 Work in groups. Put the actions in Activity 8 (on page 79) in order, where *1 = the most anti-social* and *12 = the least anti-social* action. Can you add any other anti-social actions to the list?

12 Use your list from Activity 11 to decide which of the following punishments should happen to people who are caught doing each of the things in your list.

- nothing
- a fine
- prison
- community service
- something else

Compare your decisions with those of the rest of the class.

Grammar: present modals – obligation, recommendation and permission

13 Circle the verb in blue that is the most appropriate verb in these sentences.

a Doctors have to / ought to work very long hours.
b In many countries people should / have to wear seat belts in the back of cars as well as in the front.
c You needn't / mustn't get up early if you don't want to.
d You shouldn't / mustn't use your mobile phone in here. I mean it's not against the law but it's a bit anti-social.
e You'd better not / don't have to wear a helmet when you are on your bicycle. It's your choice.
f You don't have to / ought not to play loud music. It upsets the neighbours.
g I think I'm getting fat. I hope I don't have to / shouldn't cut out chocolate.
h Bob ought not to / doesn't need to go to work since he won the lottery.

Which sentences express *1* obligation / strong advice, *2* no obligation, *3* obligation / strong advice not to do something? Check your answers with **8A–8D in the Mini-grammar.**

14 Correct the mistakes in the following sentences. Consult 8A–8D in the Mini-grammar.

a Do you must use your mobile phone in here? I don't like it.
b He was angry that he must stop talking in last night's meeting.
c I must to go to the doctor yesterday.
d We shouldn't talk in here, don't we?
e She cans not drive along this street.
f You don't need be worried.
g You had better not to play loud music at your party.
h You needn't to worry.
i You ought not drop litter.
j You shouldn't to put up posters here.

15 Sangita is 17. Complete these sentences about her using the right modals.

What do her teachers say to her?

a work harder
b try to get to school on time
c wear so much make-up
d gym is not necessary at the moment because you have exams

What does the law in Britain say?

e voting until she's 18
f 18: vote (not compulsory); go to '18 certificate' films; buy alcohol
g 17: get a full driving licence (obligatory practical and written tests)
h 16: get married; ride a moped

What does her mother say to her?

i do your homework before you go out
j don't play your music so loud
k tidy your room every Sunday (but not other days)
l wash up your own plates

Examples:

a *You must work harder.*

e *She can't vote until she is eighteen.*

k *You don't have to tidy your room every day, but you must on Sundays.*

16 Discussion **Talk about the following questions.**

a Are the laws different in your country?

Example: *In my country we can drive at sixteen.*

b What did your teachers tell you at school?

Example: *They told me I had to work harder.*

c What do you tell people who come to your house?

Example: *I tell them they must take their shoes off.*

Reading: graffiti

17 Read the text on the next page and answer the following questions.

   a What is graffiti?
   b What is most people's attitude to it?

18 **Fact check** Answer the following questions.

   a What is a tag?
   b Who are the Newcastle Two?
   c Who was sent to prison for five years?
   d Who refused to give graffiti artists walls to paint on?
   e Which tags did Simon Sunderland use?
   f Who spent £500,000 a year, and why?
   g Who complained to Simon Sunderland and what happened?
   h Who saw Simon Sunderland painting a motorway bridge?

19 **Vocabulary** Find words or phrases in the text with the following meanings. The first letter is given in each case.

   a the way people write their name, usually on a cheque or at the end of a letter (s)
   b to make or design something new for the first time (i)
   c punishments for breaking a law or rule (p)
   d actions that are against the law (o)
   e accused officially (p)
   f places (s)
   g to produce a stream of paint from a can (s)

20 **Discussion** What is your opinion about the following?

   a Graffiti – is it street art or street shame?
   b Was the judge right to send Simon Sunderland to prison?

Language in chunks

21 **Use the expressions in the box to complete the story of Bill Adams.**

according to the police	on one occasion
go to prison for a long time	things came to an end
it gives me a buzz	went up to him
it soon became clear	

Next week, 18-year-old Bill Adams goes on trial for robbery. (**a**) .... , he is one of the busiest criminals in the country.

Bill likes to rob buildings when people are in them. '(**b**) .... to take things when people are in the next room,' he told police investigators. (**c**) .... he went into a house where a party was going on. A party guest (**d**) .... and talked to him for five minutes, but Bill managed to get away from him.

However, (**e**) .... when someone saw him climbing through a window. The police arrived and arrested him. When they went to his parents' house they found hundreds of stolen items. (**f**) .... that Bill was no ordinary thief.

The police hope that Adams will (**g**) .... , but Bill remains optimistic. 'I'm young,' he said, 'I'm sure they'll give me a second chance.'

Graffiti – street art or street shame?

Tags

It all started in 1972 in New York. A painted symbol – TAKI 183 – began to appear on walls and on the side of trains. It soon became clear that TAKI 183 was the signature – or 'tag' as it is called – of a single individual who was painting anything he could. Since then, graffiti has spread all over the world, with paintings getting more and more ambitious. It is done at night on walls, bridges, public buildings and the sides of trains. Most artists have their own tag, which they keep for as long as they work – or until the police catch them. Then they have to invent a new tag for themselves.

Penalties

When the police catch graffiti artists for the first time they usually give them a small fine or a caution, but for second, third or fourth offences the penalties can get more serious.

The Newcastle Two

A few years ago, two teenagers were prosecuted in Newcastle upon Tyne in the north of England. They were sent to a young offenders' institution for three months. According to the police, they had caused £30,000 worth of damage to public property.

Simon Sunderland

Simon Sunderland was sent to prison last week for five years, one of the most serious punishments ever given to a graffiti artist. At his trial in Sheffield the judge said, 'If the people of this area could see the photographic evidence of the damage you have caused they would probably be very shocked. The message from this court is clear. If you set out to target and spray the buildings of the people of South Yorkshire, you will go to prison for a long time.'

Sunderland's career started after he asked Barnsley Council to provide walls for graffiti artists. The council refused and so he started spraying any buildings he could find using the tags 'fisto' or 'fista'. He worked at night in his favourite colours of red, black and silver. His paintings appeared on hundreds, possibly thousands, of sites. It cost the local council £500,000 a year to clean up the buildings he had painted on.

On one occasion, Sunderland sprayed a bus that had broken down. On another, a man saw him at work and went up to him to complain. Sunderland turned round and sprayed the man! In a magazine article recently he said, 'I look for walls wherever I go. It gives me a buzz. It feels like people know you!'

Things came to an end when a policeman saw him spraying a motorway bridge. When the police went to his house they discovered hundreds of spray-paint cans and maps of the areas he worked in.

What's your view?

Is graffiti ugly or is it art? Should we celebrate it or condemn it? Who should pay to have it cleaned? Should graffiti artists be sent to prison? Write to us and tell us what you think.

Functional language: asking for and giving / refusing permission

22 Before you listen to Track 45, look at the pictures and complete each conversation with one of the lines in the box.

> I'd rather you didn't.
> No, sorry. We operate a 'no dogs' policy.
> No, sir. I'm afraid taking photographs is strictly forbidden.
> Not at all. We'd love to meet her.
> Sure. Help yourself.
> Yes, certainly.

a 'Can I sit here, please?'

'..
....'

b 'Can I use my camera in here?'

'..
....'

c 'Are dogs allowed in here?'

'..
....'

d 'Is it OK if I use my mobile phone in here?'

'..
....'

e 'Is it all right if I take one of these?'

'..
....'

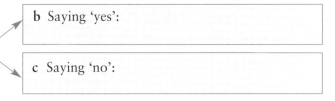

f 'Do you mind if I bring my sister to the party?'

'..
....'

Listen to Track 45. Were you correct?

23 Copy and complete the boxes with phrases from the conversations in Activity 22.

a Asking for permission:

Do you mind if I ... ?

b Saying 'yes':

c Saying 'no':

24 Which phrases from Activities 22 and 23 are:

a ... friendly?
b ... neutral?
c ... formal and official?

25 Complete the following dialogues using the expressions in Activity 23.

a '... mind if I arrive late?'
  'I'd rather ....'

b '.. right if I sit here?'
  'I'm sorry, sir, but sitting on the exhibits is strictly ....'

c '........................ I have a serviette?'
  'Sure. .... yourself.'

d 'Do .... if I take your picture?'
  'No, not .... Go ahead.'

26 Role-play Work in pairs. You are going to open a new building. Choose one of the following places and decide what rules you will make.

- art gallery
- café
- library
- nightclub
- swimming pool
- somewhere else

One of you works in the place you have chosen. The other visits as many of the places as possible around the class, and finds out what you can or can't do there using the language from Activity 23.

Writing: cohesion

27 Read the text. What is the connection between:

a ... the dog and the rabbit?
b ... Mr Jesperson and the rabbit?
c ... Mr Jesperson and the dog?
d ... Mrs Ramsey and the fence?
e ... Mr Jesperson and Harmony?
f ... Mrs Ramsey and Mr Jesperson?

Neighbour bites dog in fence dispute

1 A 47-year-old man, William Jesperson, bit <u>his</u> neighbour's dog in a dispute about <u>her</u> garden fence yesterday. Mrs Carol Ramsey has complained to the police and <u>her</u> dog needed four stitches.

2 The argument between William Jesperson and Carol Ramsey started when Mrs Ramsey took down the fence between <u>their</u> two gardens. She told <u>her</u> neighbour she was going to replace it with a newer one but she has not yet done so because, she claims, she cannot afford to.

3 When the fence was removed Mrs Ramsey's dog used Mr Jesperson's garden to play in, on one occasion frightening <u>his</u> two-year-old son, according to <u>his</u> wife Harmony. Despite repeated complaints, Mrs Ramsey did nothing, and when the dog chased Mr Jesperson's pet rabbit, the outraged father and pet lover took action.

4 Local police are investigating the incident.

28 Read the newspaper article again and answer the questions.

a What tense is used in the headline?
b Which kinds of word are missing from the headline?
c What is the purpose of each paragraph?
d Look at the underlined words. What are they?
e Who or what do each of the underlined words refer to?

29 Choose one of the topics below.

- graffiti
- street performers
- a dispute between neighbours

a Invent a story for a newspaper article about one of these topics.
b Make notes for the article showing what each paragraph should contain. How are you going to finish the article?
c Write a headline for your article.
d Write the article.

Review: grammar and functional language

30 Look at the rules for the new reference library in Charleton. Make one sentence for each rule, using a modal or semi-modal verb. Start each sentence with *You*.

Example: *You must leave coats and umbrellas at the entrance.*

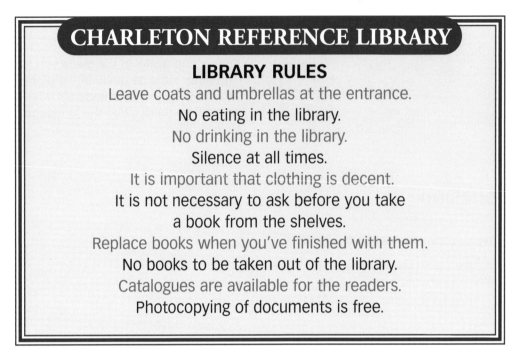

CHARLETON REFERENCE LIBRARY

LIBRARY RULES
Leave coats and umbrellas at the entrance.
No eating in the library.
No drinking in the library.
Silence at all times.
It is important that clothing is decent.
It is not necessary to ask before you take
a book from the shelves.
Replace books when you've finished with them.
No books to be taken out of the library.
Catalogues are available for the readers.
Photocopying of documents is free.

31 Work in pairs. Write four sentences with gaps to test your partner's knowledge of modal verbs.

Example: *You .... wear a uniform at work. It's up to you.*
(You don't have to wear a uniform at work. It's up to you.)

32 Complete the phrases and sentences. Then match the requests and replies in the two columns.

a .... I use my Walkman in here?
b Are children .... in here?
c Do you .... if I take one of these biscuits?
d Is it .... if I take photographs?

e No, madam, I'm afraid it .... Taking photographs is strictly forbidden.
f No you .... We have a silence rule and that thing would make a noise.
g Not at all! .... yourself.
h Yes, of .... You can go into the family room.

Where do you think all these exchanges take place?

Review: vocabulary

anti-social   community service   dispute
fine (n)   graffiti   invent   ma'am
offence   law   papers   penalty
permission   permit   precinct   prison
prosecute   rule   signature   site
spray (v)   spray-paint (v)

according to the police   to let your dog foul the
it gives me a buzz   footpath
on one occasion   to light a smoky
things came to an end   bonfire / barbecue
to become clear   to make a lot of noise
to drop litter   to put up posters
to go up to somebody

33 Which five words or phrases from the Word List and Word Plus would you use most in an English-speaking country? Why? Give examples of how you might use them.

Pronunciation

34 a Find words in the Word List and Word Plus with the same sound as each of the following words, and write them in the correct column

/aɪ/ – fine	/aɪə/ – liar	/ɪə/- fear

Listen to Track 46 and check.
Try to add more words of your own in each column in the table.

b Write sentences which accuse people of performing anti-social acts. Use the words from the Word List and Word Plus as in this example:

You dropped litter on the pavement.

Mark where you would put the stresses in the sentences, like this:

You dropped litter on the pavement.

35 Use the following diagram as a start for your own 'wordmap' about anti-social behaviour. Use words from the Word List (and any others you know) to extend the 'wordmap' as far as possible.

drop litter

ride bicycles on the pavement

mess

anti-social behaviour

danger

36 Writing Imagine you are a judge in a courtroom. Using the words from Word Plus, write a speech addressing someone who has been found guilty of anti-social behaviour. Look back at the reading text on page 83, to help you. Read your speech to the class.

Example: *Maria Shockley, according to the police, you let your dog foul the footpath even though it is against the law, and so I fine you £100.*

Body talk

→ describing nouns
→ body language
→ giving signs with body language

Reading: what body language means

1 Look at the pictures *a–f* below. How are the people feeling? How do you know?

2 Read the text and match the pictures to the gestures that are mentioned.

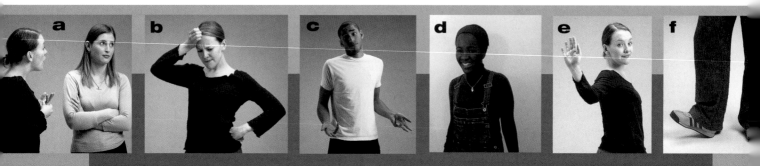

Talking bodies

We know what our words mean, but how good are we at understanding body language?
Sarah Frost reports

When you talk to people face to face, you communicate with much more than your words and the sound of your voice. You also give an enormous amount of information through the language of your body. In fact, in any communication, over 50 per cent of the information you give comes from your body language. We all use body language, whether consciously or subconsciously, and it can tell people more about us than we might want them to know.

The use of body language can be a powerful indicator of how you feel. This is often a conscious way of communicating. Smiling shows you are happy; shrugging your shoulders tells someone that you don't know something or that you don't care, and waving is a way of saying 'hello' or 'goodbye'. There are other gestures, however, that give information without you realising. Crossing your arms may indicate that you are relaxed, bored or want to protect yourself; scratching your head might show you are puzzled; tapping your foot might mean you are feeling impatient, and fidgeting might show you are nervous.

When people are good friends or when two people agree with each other, they often echo each other's body language, crossing their legs in the same way or using the same gestures. This is often done subconsciously but a person might copy someone else's body movements consciously to make fun of them!

How often you look into someone's eyes also sends powerful messages. We make eye contact more often in a conversation with friends than with strangers and lack of eye contact can indicate nervousness. In general conversation, we look at each other for short periods of time, but when the topic becomes more personal we often look away. Deep eye contact is usually only used for very strong emotions such as love or anger. If someone avoids eye contact altogether when speaking, it might mean they are not telling the truth.

The physical distance between speakers can indicate a number of things. Standing close together, for example, can suggest intimacy, whilst distance may indicate formality or a lack of interest. Standing close to someone may be quite appropriate in some situations, such as an informal party, but completely out of place in others, such as a meeting with your boss.

Body language can sometimes get you into trouble when you travel abroad. Smiling is an almost universal signal of pleasure or welcome, but other gestures may have different meanings in different cultures. The same gesture, used in different cultures, can mean 'OK', 'zero', 'fantastic result', 'money' – or something much more insulting! In Britain, people often raise their eyebrows to suggest surprise or interest; when they bite their lip we think they may be uncertain or worried; when they clench their teeth or their fist we know they are angry.

So when you next talk to somebody – be careful. Your body may be saying a lot more than you think!

3 Match these words from the text with the following meanings.

> universal subconsciously protect yourself
> strangers intimacy uncertain fidgeting

a a close personal relationship
b all over the world
c confused
d making a lot of small, restless movements, usually with your hands
e people we don't know
f to do something without being aware
g to make yourself safe from danger

4 Fact check **According to the text, why might people:**

a ... smile?
b ... raise their eyebrows?
c ... bite their lips?
d ... shrug their shoulders?
e ... cross their arms?
f ... wave?
g ... scratch their head?

5 Comprehension **Look at the text again and answer these questions.**

a How might the topic of conversation affect how much eye contact you make?
b How does your relationship with the person you are talking to affect the physical distance between you?
c How and why do people echo each other's body language?
d Why could using certain gestures in another country get you into trouble?

Language in chunks

6 Match the phrases in the first column with their opposites in the second column.

> face-to-face   appropriate
> out of place   lying
> telling the truth   without seeing the people we're talking to

7 Complete the following sentences with the correct expression from Activity 6.

a Before we go on, I need to know that you are ....
b Look, it would be much easier if we talked .... rather than on the phone.
c I feel really .... here. Can we go home?

Vocabulary: body language

Using a dictionary: verb collocation

8 Look at this dictionary entry for *clench*.

small, sweet orang—
clench /klentʃ/ v [T] **1 clench your fists/teeth/jaw** etc to hold your hands, teeth etc together tightly, usually because you feel angry or determined: *Jody was pacing the sidelines, her fists clenched.* **2** to hold something tightly in your hand or between your teeth: *a cigar clenched between his teeth*
—v /ˈklɜːdʒi   n the clergy [plural] the

a Does the verb always take an object? How do you know?
b What nouns is it used with most often?

9 Using a dictionary, choose a noun from the second list that is often used with these verbs. Sometimes there is more than one answer.

Verbs   **Nouns**

a clench + ...   arms
b cross   + ...   ear
c fold   + ...   eyebrows
d nod   + ...   finger(s)
e point   + ...   fist
f raise   + ...   hand(s)
g scratch + ...   head
h shake   + ...   legs
i shrug   + ...   neck
j wag   + ...   shoulders
k wave   + ...   teeth

10 Look at the picture and say who:

a .... has folded his arms.
b .... is clenching his fist.
c .... is wagging its tail.
d .... has crossed his legs.
e .... is raising her eyebrows.
f .... is pointing at someone.
g .... is waving her arms.
h .... is nodding his head.
i .... is scratching his head.
j .... is shrugging her shoulders.

11 Complete the sentences using a verb and noun pair from Activity 9. Change the verb to the -ing form and add a possessive adjective (e.g. his, her).

a 'Get your dog out of my garden!' Mr King shouted,
   ...shaking his fist.. .

b 'Yes, you're right,' Louise agreed,
   ....

c 'Look, it's over there,' Juan said,
   ....

d 'I don't really care,' Carla said,
   ....

e 'This is a really comfortable chair!' the customer said,
   ....

f 'Goodbye,' Frank said,
   ....

g 'You are a very naughty girl!' the teacher said,
   ....

h 'Oh dear. I just don't understand how it works,' the technician
   said, ...

i 'Ooh! That's a surprise,' Barbara said,
   ....

j 'I must try to be patient,' Janine thought,
   ....

12 What gestures do people use in your country to do the following?

a say 'hello': ....

b say 'goodbye': ....

c express agreement: ....

d express anger: ....

e express boredom: ....

f express relaxation: ....

g express disagreement: ....

h express indifference: ....

i express surprise: ....

●●● Pronunciation:
how many syllables?

13 Listen to Track 47 and write down how many syllables you hear for each word.

a different
b interest
c usually
d consciously
e general
f intimacy
g subconsciously
h relaxation

14 Find more three- and four-syllable words in this unit.

Speaking: test your memory

15 Look at the picture. Give yourself exactly 50 seconds. Try to remember everything in it.

Now cover the picture. In pairs discuss how much you remember, and write down what you discussed.

16 Look at the picture again. Who remembered the most details correctly?

Functional language: using gesture to express meaning

17 Look at the pictures. How do you think the people feel about each other and the conversations they are having. How do you know?

18 Think of someone you would like to interview for a newspaper article or TV interview. Write in the table seven interview questions that you could use.

Examples: What kind of music do you like?

What has been the most important moment in your career so far?

Question 1:	
Question 2:	
Question 3:	
Question 4:	
Question 5:	
Question 6:	
Question 7:	

19 Work in pairs.

a Give your partner your questions for the person you have chosen. Your partner uses the questions to interview you as if you were that person. You can use your imagination for your answers.

b Choose a letter between *a* and *m*. Look at Activity Bank 5 on page 152 to find the letter which shows how you are feeling. Repeat the interview, but this time show how you are feeling using body language and tone of voice. Your interviewer has to guess which letter you chose.

Listening: line-up

20 Look at the picture. Why are the men there?

21 Listen to Track 48. Which man *1–7* does the woman choose?

22 Fact check Listen to Track 48 again. Answer the questions.

   a How did the woman get to the police station?
   b What did someone take from her?
   c What does the woman say about her eyes?
   d Why is she unsure about the identity of the thief?

23 Which word fits in all of the gaps in the following extract?

POLICEMAN: Well, who is it?

   WOMAN: That ....

POLICEMAN: Which .... ?

   WOMAN: The .... with the beard.

POLICEMAN: There are three men with beards.

   WOMAN: Yes.

POLICEMAN: So which .... is it? Please.

   WOMAN: The tall man in a green jacket.

POLICEMAN: Yes, but there are two men with green ...

   WOMAN: Look! That ....

POLICEMAN: Which .... ?

   WOMAN: The .... scratching his ear.

Check your answer with Track 48.

24 Cover the picture. Now write a description of man number 3. Compare your descriptions. Are you good witnesses?

Grammar: noun phrases

25 Find the words or phrases in the box which could be used to modify the nouns in blue in the following sentences.

at the side of the building	membership
temporary	without a card
at the desk	valuable
in the blue uniform	horrible
sports	dangerous

   a The man stopped Jenny as she went into the club.
     the man in the blue uniform
   b 'Have you got your card?' he said.
   c Jenny looked in her bag, but she couldn't find it.
   d 'I'm afraid I can't let anyone into the club,' he said.
   e Somebody has damaged a lot of equipment.
   f 'But you know it wasn't me! I'm not a criminal!' she said.
   g 'Well, you can get a card from the desk,' he said, smiling.
   h 'Thank you,' she said, 'the girl will recognise me, I'm sure.'
   i Jenny followed the man through a door.
   j 'Why would anyone do such a thing?' she wondered.

Look at 9A and 9B in the Mini-grammar, to check your answers.

26 Match the first and second half of each headline. The first one is done for you.

a Government closes cancer   1 ... written by son
b Father attacks book   2 ... parked outside embassy
c Lawyer defends politician   3 ... ward in local hospital
d Mother searches for son   4 ... bitten by dog
e Photographer films woman   5 ... sleeping in class
f Police blow up car   6 ... accused of taking money
g Swimmer frees dolphin   7 ... with memory loss
h Thieves steal picture   8 ... accused of shoplifting
i Teachers find more pupils   9 ... painted by Rembrandt
j Ambulance crew helps boy   10 ... caught in net

27 Complete the following news stories by adding the information in the boxes. Use either the present participle or the past participle after each noun.

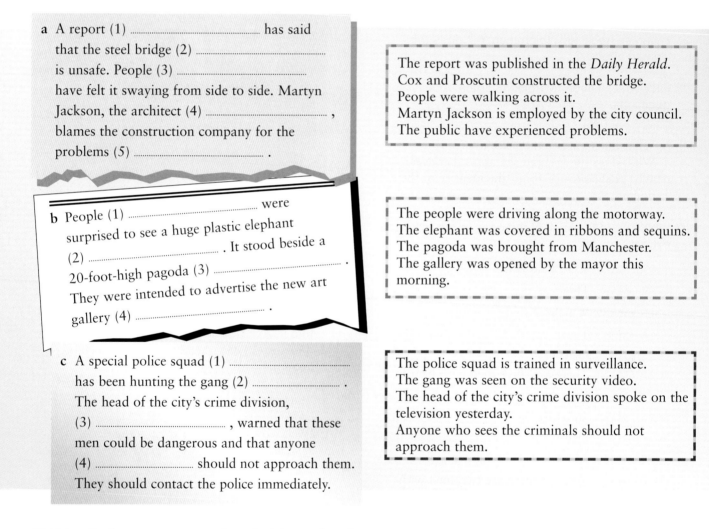

a A report (1) .... has said
   that the steel bridge (2) ....
   is unsafe. People (3) ....
   have felt it swaying from side to side. Martyn
   Jackson, the architect (4) .... ,
   blames the construction company for the
   problems (5) ....

The report was published in the *Daily Herald*.
Cox and Proscutin constructed the bridge.
People were walking across it.
Martyn Jackson is employed by the city council.
The public have experienced problems.

b People (1) .... were
   surprised to see a huge plastic elephant
   (2) .... It stood beside a
   20-foot-high pagoda (3) ....
   They were intended to advertise the new art
   gallery (4) ....

The people were driving along the motorway.
The elephant was covered in ribbons and sequins.
The pagoda was brought from Manchester.
The gallery was opened by the mayor this morning.

c A special police squad (1) ....
   has been hunting the gang (2) ....
   The head of the city's crime division,
   (3) .... , warned that these
   men could be dangerous and that anyone
   (4) .... should not approach them.
   They should contact the police immediately.

The police squad is trained in surveillance.
The gang was seen on the security video.
The head of the city's crime division spoke on the television yesterday.
Anyone who sees the criminals should not approach them.

28 Using the language patterns from Activity 27 describe a famous person or someone in the class. The others have to guess who it is.

Examples: *I'm thinking of a young person with blue eyes – in this classroom!*

I'm thinking of a woman married to a footballer. She's a singer with a pop group.

Writing: written statements

29 Read the witness statement. It was written by the police officer who interviewed John Burney. The police officer wrote the statement in the first person (I = John Burney). John Burney will be asked to sign the statement. Answer the questions.

a What crime took place?
b How many people were involved?

WITNESS STATEMENT FORM

NAME: John Burney
ADDRESS: 32 Albert Close, Glasgow, GL2 1BT

STATEMENT

I was in the bank at 12.30. I saw two men and a girl run into the bank. A tall, white man with a gun ran up to the window and shouted something like 'Give me all your money'. He had short, dark hair. A second man, with a suitcase, went up to the window and helped the first man to put money into it. He was a 30-year-old, black man wearing jeans and a black sweater. He was very tall. The girl was about 25 with long blonde hair, wearing red trousers and a white shirt. When the suitcase was full I saw all three of them run out of the bank.

Signed: ....   Date: ....

30 Listen to Track 49. John Burney (the witness) is describing the scene to a police officer. What three mistakes has the police officer made?

31 Look at the picture. Write a conversation, like the one on Track 49, between someone who saw the event and the police officer who is interviewing them.

32 Using the conversation you have written, write a 'witness statement' like the one in Activity 29.

Review: grammar and vocabulary

33 Read the following passage. What words and phrases describe the nouns in blue?

We went to a lovely party given by the old man from number 27 last night. We really enjoyed the meal cooked by his eldest son.

We then moved into the elegant sitting room. It had blue walls covered with expensive paintings. Suddenly there was a knock at the front door. The neighbour from number 29 went to answer it, but when she opened the old, green door, two men wearing masks ran past her and came into the room.

It was terrifying. One of the men was carrying a shotgun with two long barrels, and he told us he'd kill us immediately if we moved a muscle. So we just sat there as they took the biggest paintings in the house and wrapped them in a large piece of white cloth. Then they ran out and got into a van parked in front of the house.

We rang the police and two young officers arrived in two minutes from the local police station. They asked us long and detailed questions.

The tall policeman with the big moustache told us they would do everything they could to catch the thieves.

Examples: party – lovely (a lovely party)
party – given by the old man (a party given by the old man)

34 Expand these sentences by putting words and phrases before and after the nouns to describe them.

a A driving instructor was talking to a man.
A young driving instructor with blond hair and a beard was talking to a tall man.

b The bank manager looked at the bank notes.
c The boy bought a new calculator.
d The café was in a street.
e The dog knocked over the computer.
f The executive had always wanted a mobile phone.
g The girl was reading a poem.
h The man had his first driving lesson.
i The police officer found a photograph.
j The violinist played the music.
k The woman pointed to the suspect.

35 Look at these people. What are they doing? What does the action mean? How do you think they feel?

Example: Paul's waving his arm. He's saying goodbye to someone. He feels sad.

Review: vocabulary

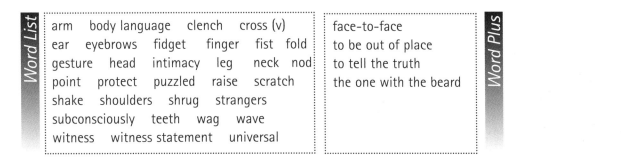

Word List

arm   body language   clench   cross (v)
ear   eyebrows   fidget   finger   fist   fold
gesture   head   intimacy   leg   neck   nod
point   protect   puzzled   raise   scratch
shake   shoulders   shrug   strangers
subconsciously   teeth   wag   wave
witness   witness statement   universal

Word Plus

face-to-face
to be out of place
to tell the truth
the one with the beard

36 Find at least three words from the Word List which have more than one meaning.

●●● Pronunciation

37 a How many different sounds does each of the following words have?
Which is the easiest / most difficult word to pronounce?

1 cross ....4............

2 finger ....

3 indifference ....

4 puzzled ....

5 strangers ....

6 truth ....

⊕ Listen to Track 50 and check.

b Find words in the Word List with four syllables. Where is the main stress?

⊕ Listen to Track 51 and check.

What other words can you think of with the same stress patterns?

38 When you look at people, how do you know if they:

a ... are telling a lie?
b ... are puzzled?
c ... are feeling impatient?

UNIT 10
Technocrazy

→ defining relative clauses
→ computers
→ asking for technical help

Speaking: reaching agreement

1 **Vocabulary** Match the words with the items in the picture.

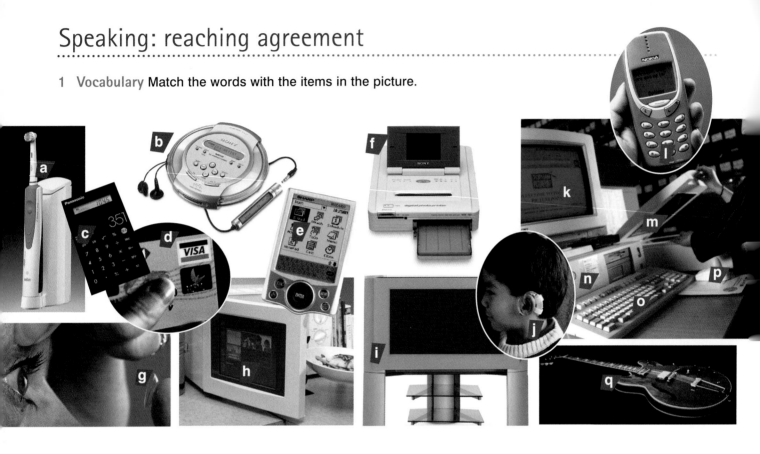

calculator	[ ]	electric toothbrush	[ ]	monitor	[ ]
computer	[ ]	electronic personal		mouse	[ ]
contact lenses	[ ]	organiser	[ ]	personal stereo	[ ]
credit card	[ ]	keyboard	[ ]	printer	[ ]
hearing aid	[ ]	microwave oven	[ ]	scanner	[ ]
electric guitar	[ ]	mobile phone	[ ]	television	[ ]

2 Put the items in order of importance, where *1 = most important to you* and *17 = least important to you*. Compare your list with a partner's.

3 **Discussion** Which invention do you think should win the prize for being the greatest invention of the 20th century? It can be one of the things from Activity 1 or a completely different invention.

Reading: Are computers a waste of money?

4 Discuss the following questions.

• Why do schools need computers?
• What are computers most useful for?

5 Read the text opposite. Does the writer agree with you?

Wired? Not worth it!

Convinced that your kids will be left behind unless they become computer experts? Anxious that their school doesn't have enough computers? Well, don't be! Theodore Roszak has 12 reasons why computers are definitely not a good idea.

1 Don't believe all the hype from the people who sell computers. They are just trying to sell more merchandise, and you can't always believe their claims.

2 People who say that schools need more computers are like doctors who prescribe medicine when the patient doesn't really need it.

3 By the time a school decides to buy a computer, it will be out of date. The manufacturers keep bringing out new models, and the old ones soon become outmoded.

4 The money schools use to buy computers could often be better spent on things that are more necessary – for example teachers' salaries, musical instruments or fixing the roof.

5 Whatever kids learn about computers in primary school, it won't be much use when they eventually get a job. Different firms have different computer systems, and employers should teach employees what they need to know after they hire them.

6 Computers don't create more jobs – they reduce the amount of work available. If we could get rid of computers right now, there would be many more jobs available for people to do!

7 Playing computer games is not the same as learning. Of course, games are fun – there's nothing wrong with that. But traditional learning teaches children many more important skills, such as concentrating for long periods of time, questioning things and developing memory.

8 As soon as you spend money on a computer, you will need to carry on spending just to keep up to date. (That's a lot of money down the drain!)

9 People who are computer enthusiasts often say that computers are educational, and rave about all the information the Internet can offer children. But beware if they tell you that information is everything. Information is only the answer to a question – it is the kind of question you ask that is important.

10 Learning isn't just about gathering information; it also means finding out about all kinds of ideas, values, tastes and opinions. Books offer the best ways of finding out about these things. Let your kids learn from all that authors and teachers have to offer.

11 The Internet is basically a huge advertising system. If a school asked for all advertising to be taken off the Internet, the manufacturers would tell them it was impossible. It isn't.

12 It is a myth that all children born since 1990 have an innate ability to use computers. Give a child a piece of paper and a pencil, and they will immediately draw or write something. But sit a young child in front of a computer, and he won't know where to begin!

---

6 Find which paragraph in the text says the opposite of the following statements.

a A good computer system will last for a long time. *paragraph 3*
b Computer manufacturers are honest about what the machines do.
c Computers are better sources of information than books.
d Computer games help to teach children important skills.
e Schools always need more computers, just as a patient always needs medicine.
f School money is best spent on computers.
g Information is more important than asking the right questions.
h Most kids today find using computers easy.
i Once you've bought a computer system you won't have to spend any more money.
j Computers create jobs.
k Good computer skills learned in primary school will help children get a job when they grow up.
l The Internet doesn't have any advertisements on it.

7 Look at these words from the text on page 99. Tick the words you know and then complete the tasks below.

> hype ▧   myth ▧   prescribe ▧   kids ▧
>
> enthusiasts ▧   wired ▧   salaries ▧
>
> innate ▧   outmoded ▧

a Find out the meaning of the words you did not tick in a dictionary.

b Use the new words in sentences.

8 Write your answer to one of the following questions.

a Has Theodore Roszak's article changed your opinion about computers in schools? Explain your answer.

b Theodore Roszak wrote this article in 1996. Is what it says still true in your opinion?

Compare your answers with other students'.

9 **Noticing language** What word follows each of these nouns in the text? What follows the word?

a people (reason 1)

b people (reason 2)

c things (reason 4)

d people (reason 9)

Language in chunks

10 Put the following words in the right order to make phrases from the text.

a a / not / idea / good

b time / the/by

c date / of / out

d that / with / wrong / nothing

e periods / of / long

f drain / the / down

g about / raves

11 Complete the following sentences with the appropriate phrases from Activity 10.

a .... you get home your dinner will be ready.

b Having another piece of cake is definitely .... You've had three pieces already.

c November 1999? These magazines are ....

d If you want to be a bird-watcher, expect .... boredom.

e Sue really likes that new American rock band. She .... the singer all the time!

f You want to buy a new computer? There's .... , except that you have got two already.

g I bought a new skirt last week, but it has split already. That's more money ....

Grammar: relative clauses (defining)

12 Put the correct pronoun (*that*, *which*, *who*, *whose*, *when* or *where*) in the gaps in the following sentences.

a He's the man .... won the lottery.

b That's the dog .... chased me in the park.

c Shall we buy the sofa .... we saw in the window yesterday?

d The village .... Alain lived is in Normandy.

e Everyone celebrated that day .... the agreement was signed.

f The café .... has Internet access is on George Street.

g Who is the person .... ordered the pizza?

h Which is the street .... the museum is?

i The book .... has a yellow cover is a murder mystery.

j The woman .... basement was flooded has left the area.

Check your answers by looking at **10A in the Mini-grammar**.

13 Look again at **10A** in the **Mini-grammar** – particularly at the difference between subject and object pronouns, and at when we do not have to use a pronoun. Now decide which of these sentences are correct.

a He's the man she married.

b He's the man met her at a party.

c They're the people invited us to their party.

d They're the people we have known for three years.

e That's the ring was lost.

f That's the ring he gave her.

What relative pronouns can you use in each of these sentences?

14 Complete the sentences with an appropriate relative pronoun. Do not use one if it is not necessary.

a The other day I bumped into a woman .... I used to go to school with.

b I will never forget some of the people .... went to that school.

c She suggested going to a restaurant .... she knew.

d We sat at a table .... was in a dark corner.

e The waiter .... served us seemed very friendly.

f My friend started talking in a whisper. She told me about some criminals .... she knew.

g She said they were people .... used computers to rob banks.

h I couldn't believe the information .... she gave me.

i I took my mobile phone from the bag .... my boyfriend had given me, and made a phone call.

j The person I called was a friend .... had recently been promoted to sergeant in the police force.

k On the way out of the restaurant I was stopped by a man .... expression was not friendly. It was the nice waiter.

l 'You're not the kind of person .... we want in this restaurant,' he growled.

m I looked for the friend .... had brought me here. But she had gone.

15 Work in pairs. Student A, look at Activity Bank 11 on page 154. Student B, look at Activity Bank 17 on page 157.

16 Complete the sentences with relative clauses. You can change words to make the sentences more personal if you want.

a Drivers ...who drive too slowly... are very annoying.

b He wanted to wear the jacket ....

c I can still remember the photograph ....

d I don't like people ....

e I like food ....

f Last week I met someone ....

g My friends like the kind of music ....

h She will never forget the competition ....

i The book .... was very interesting.

j The film director .... was seen in a restaurant with the star of his last film.

Vocabulary: computers

17 Using a dictionary if you need to, complete the sentences with words or phrases from the box.

> computer viruses   crashes   emails
> bug   go online   website

a You can't .... if your brother is using the telephone line to talk to his friends.

b Many people send and receive .... rather than telephoning or using 'snail mail' (letter post).

c These days you can buy things on the Internet by going to a company's ....

d Sometimes the computer .... , and then it's impossible to use it. You usually have to switch it off and start again.

e Some people create .... , which infect any computer they arrive at. They are very dangerous and can destroy everything on the hard disk.

f If a computer programme has a .... , it won't work properly.

18 Look at the dictionary entry for *application*.

application /ˌæplɪˈkeɪʃn/ noun ★★★

1 request for sth	**4** effort/determination
2 particular use sth has	**5** putting sth onto surface
3 computer software	

1 [C/U] a formal request for permission to do or have something: **+for** *His application for membership of the club was rejected.* ♦ **application to do sth** *The hospital submitted a planning application to build four new wards.* ♦ **make/submit/put in an application** *I'm supposed to submit my application before the end of the week.* ♦ **grant/approve an application** *The building society has approved their mortgage application.* **1a.** a written request for a job or a place at a college, university etc: *The university welcomes applications from mature students.* ♦ *a letter of application*
2 [C] a particular use that something has: *the practical applications of this technology* **2a.** [U] the use of a particular method, process, law etc: *He pioneered the application of scientific techniques to police work.*
3 [C] *computing* a piece of computer software that is designed to do a particular job
4 [U] *formal* hard work and determination that you put into something for a long period: *With the right degree of application and dedication the team should win a medal.*
5 [C/U] the process of putting a substance such as paint or glue onto a surface

a How many different meanings are given?
b Is the noun countable (like *table* – we can say *a table*, *two tables*, etc.) or uncountable (like *furniture* – we can't say ~~two furnitures~~)? How do you know?
c What words follow *application* in meaning 1?
d What do you know about meanings 3 and 4? When is *application* used for these meanings?

19 Put the following computer operations in the correct place in the flow chart.

- Close the application.
- Open the application you want.
- Print your work.
- Save your work onto the hard disk.
- Switch off the computer, the monitor and the printer.
- Switch on the computer, the monitor and the printer.
- Work.

a **Switch on the computer, the monitor and the printer.**

↓

b

↓

c

↓

d

↓

e

↓

f

↓

g

20 Imagine that a software company has asked you to conduct a survey about how people use computers. Write six questions for the survey. You can use some or all of the verbs in the box, any language from this section, and any other language from the unit.

have	print	receive	save
send	suffered from	use	

Examples: How often do you use a scanner?

Has your computer ever had a computer virus?

21 Use your questions from Activity 20 to interview other members of the class.

Functional language: asking for (technical) help

22 Read all the conversations and then decide where these questions and replies should go in them.

> do you know how to connect up to the Internet?
> Have you checked the connection
> How may I help you?
> No. Do you think that will help?
> OK. I'll give it a try.
> Really?
> Thanks. That's great!
> Well, I can't get my personal organiser to work with my computer.

a

RON: Computer Helpline, Ron speaking.

KARL: Oh, hello. Can you help me?

RON: What's the problem?

KARL: **(1)** ....

RON: OK. Have you checked the batteries in your organiser?

KARL: Yes, of course.

RON: **(2)** .... at the back of your computer?

KARL: **(3)** ....

RON: Do I think it will help? Well why don't you try and see?

b

RACHEL: Hello. Computer Helpline. Rachel speaking. What seems to be the problem?

JIM: Umm, well I know this is silly, but **(1)** .... ?

RACHEL: What system are you using?

JIM: It's an Apple Mac.

RACHEL: OK. Do you have an Internet icon on your screen? Like a globe?

JIM: Yes. Yes, I do.

RACHEL: Well then, just click on the icon and you're away.

JIM: OK, ... oh yes. **(2)** ....

RACHEL: You're welcome.

c

MIKE: Hi, Computer Helpline. My name's Mike. **(1)** .... ?

MILLIE: This thing is driving me crazy!

MIKE: Hold on! What's the problem?

MILLIE: Well, my computer seems to have crashed.

MIKE: How exactly?

MILLIE: Well, I can't move anything. Even the cursor just sticks in the same place.

MIKE: OK, well the best thing to do is to switch off and start again.

MILLIE: **(2)** ....

MIKE: Yes, really. That's what I would do.

MILLIE: **(3)** .... Thanks.

MIKE: No problem.

🔊 Now listen to Track 52. Were you correct?

23 Put the following lines from the conversations on page 103 in the right columns.

Do you think that will help?
Can you help me?
Do you know how to connect up to the Internet?
Have you checked the batteries?
Just click on the icon.
OK. I'll give it a try.
Really?
Thanks.

That's great.
That's what I would do.
The best thing to do is to switch off and start again.
This thing is driving me crazy.
Why don't you try and see?
What seems to be the problem?

a Asking for help / stating a problem:	b Giving help / advice:	c Responding to help / advice:
		Do you think that will help?

· ·

Pronunciation:
fluent speech

24 Listen to the two speakers on Track 53. Which one do you think speaks more fluently, the man or the woman?

25 When the more fluent speaker is talking on Track 53, which words run into each other and change their sounds? When words run into each other use a curved line (⌣). When sounds change, use a straight line (—).

a Can you help me?
b What seems to be the problem?
c Have you checked the batteries?
d Do you know how to use this answerphone?
e What is the problem?
f What do I do now?

26 Say the questions like the woman on Track 53.

27 Write the replies (in the box) that match with the sentences below. Use each reply once only.

Is it plugged in?
You're welcome.
Sure. Just press the red button and record your message.
The best thing to do would be to call the garage.
Well, that's what I would do.
Why? What seems to be the problem?

a 'Do you know how to use this answerphone?'
'...'

b 'Do you think it will work?'
'...'

c 'My car won't start.' '...'

d 'My iron doesn't work. It's not even hot.'
'...'

e 'Thanks very much for your help.'
'...'

f 'This photocopier is driving me crazy.'
'...'

28 Work in pairs. Write conversations in which one of you has a problem to which the other knows the answer. You can write about one of the following.

- a computer
- a mobile phone
- a stereo
- a car
- an iron

- a camera
- a photocopier
- an answerphone
- a microwave

Act out your conversations for the class.

Listening: the news

29 Listen to Track 54. Which of the following topics are discussed in the news broadcast? Tick those that are mentioned in the first column.

a company collapse   [   ]   [   ]
b computer virus   [   ]   [   ]
c cure for cancer discovered   [   ]   [   ]
d earthquake   [   ]   [   ]
e election results   [   ]   [   ]
f Internet romance   [   ]   [   ]
g mountain rescue   [   ]   [   ]
h peace talks   [   ]   [   ]
i plane crash   [   ]   [   ]
j rocket launch for Pluto expedition [   ]   [   ]

In the second column above, number the stories that you have ticked in the order that you hear them.

30 **Fact check** Listen to Track 54 again, and then write answers to the questions. What is the connection between:

a ... a mobile phone and a mountain?
b ... K2 and Paris?
c ... a computer virus and Puerto Rico?
d ... Bella Karsfield and 'Money for jam'?
e ... Oxford and Tuscaloosa?
f ... young and 65?
g ... $70 million and holiday homes?

31 Answer the following questions about the news reports.

a Who was saved from almost certain death?
b Where were there appalling weather conditions?
c Who got over his surprise?
d Who is trying to trace the source of what?
e Who eventually agreed to marry?
f Who had lied about her age?
g Who or what is to cease business?
h Who expects more business failures?

32 Retell the story of one of the news items, but make at least two deliberate mistakes about who the people are, where they are, what happened, etc. (Refer to Track 54 in the Audioscript.) The others have to spot your mistakes and correct them.

Example: STUDENT A: *A French woman was saved from almost certain death when she called her boyfriend on her mobile phone.*

STUDENT B: *It wasn't her boyfriend. It was her husband.*

Writing: TXT MSGNG

The biggest growth in mobile phone use in the last five years has been text messaging. In these messages people use a special kind of language because they want to write quickly.

33 Match the text messages on the left with their meanings on the right.

a 2DAY
b ATB
c B48
d BCNU
e BTW
f CUL8R
g GR8
h LOL
i LUV
j NE1
k NO1
l OIC
m RUOK
n SOME1
o THX
p WAN2
q WKND
r XOXOXOXOX

all the best
anyone
Are you OK?
by the way
great
lots of love
love
love and kisses
no one
Oh I see.
See you later.
someone
thanks
before eight
today
want to
be seeing you
weekend

34 What do the following text messages mean? Can you translate them into ordinary English?

a

> Do U wan2 cum out with me?
> Andy

b

> Clown's Caf?
> Andy

c

> Fantastic! CU 2moro
> Andy

d

> Gr8!!!
> Andy

e

> O Pls. Just 1ns.
> Andy

f

> 2moro? CU about 8?
> Andy

g

> OK. CU then.
> Jill

h

> No thx.
> Jill

i

> Where?
> Jill

j

> When?
> Jill

k

> OK. Just 1ns.
> Jill

Now put the messages in order. Andy's message (a) starts the sequence.

1 .... 2 .... 3 .... 4 .... 5 .... 6 ....

7 .... 8 .... 9 .... 10 .... 11 ....

35 Andy and Jill met up as a result of their text messages in Activity 34. Write the text messages they sent each other the next day.

Examples:

> Thx 4 lovely eve.
> CU on Tuesday.
>
> Jill XXX

> Sorry about what I said.
> Can I CU L8TR?
>
> Andy

Review: grammar and functional language

36 Read the text and complete the exercise which follows.

Jake Houseman decided to be a computer wizard, so he first went and asked his brother Martin for advice. Martin was out, so he asked his other brother, Paul, what to do. Paul told him about a shop called Computer Solutions, which was very cheap, so he went there and bought a 'Century' (a very new type of computer).

As he was taking the boxes from the car, his neighbour Geraldine (from the house on the left) asked him what he had bought. Then Roy, Geraldine's dog, bit him on the left leg and he dropped the printer on his foot. He went to see his doctor, Miriam Barrett, and she told him to go to hospital. When he got there, another doctor, Jacky Sewell, told him he had nothing to worry about and sent him home. When he got home, his other neighbour Gloria (from the house on the right) asked him if she could use his new computer. He agreed, but Gloria's dog Rex bit his other leg and once again he had to go back to hospital. This time a third doctor, Jordan Freeman, gave him a bed and he spent the night there.

When he woke up the next morning, he thought about the previous day's events. He realised that he had learned something useful. 'What yesterday's events have taught me,' he thought, 'is that ... .'

Make sentences about the following people, places and animals using *who*, *which*, *that* and *whose*.

Martin	Century	Jacky Sewell
Paul	Geraldine	Gloria
Computer Solutions	Roy	Rex
	Miriam Barrett	Jordan Freeman

Example: Martin is the brother who was out.

37 Complete Jake's thought at the end of the text in Activity 36. Compare your version with a partner's. Are they the same?

38 Match the questions and phrases on the left with the answers on the right.

a Can you help me?
b What can you suggest to make this computer work?
c Have you checked the batteries?
d Thanks very much.
e The best thing is to start again.
f This machine is driving me crazy.
g What seems to be the problem?

1 Have you tried switching it off and going for a walk?
2 OK. I'll give it a try
3 Sure. What seems to be the problem?
4 The photocopier isn't working.
5 Well, I'd switch it on first.
6 Yes. They're new. They're fine.
7 You're welcome.

Review: vocabulary

Word List

calculator   computer   computer bug
computer virus   contact lenses
credit card   electric guitar
electric toothbrush   electronic personal organiser
emails   enthusiasts   go online   hard disk
hearing aid   hype   innate   invention   keyboard
kid   microwave oven   mobile phone   modem
monitor   myth   outmoded   personal stereo
prescribe   printer   salary   scanner   television
text message   website   wired

Word Plus

appalling weather conditions
by the time
down the drain
long periods of
not a good idea
nothing wrong with that
out of date
the computer's crashed
the first step towards

to agree to marry
to be saved from almost certain death
to get over (your) surprise
to lie about (your) age
to rave about (something)
to trace the source of something

39 Look at the words in the Word List. Underline the words which are connected with computers. Which of them are like words in your language? Which are completely different?

Pronunciation

40 a Copy and complete the table with words from the Word List that match the stress pattern. The circles represent the syllables. The large circle represents the stressed syllable.

1 oOo	2 Ooo	3 ooOo	4 Oooo
electric		television	

Listen to Track 55 and check.

b Find examples of words from the Word List and Word Plus with the following consonant clusters.

1 /kr/ cricket	2 /sk/ school	3 /tr/ travel

Listen to Track 56 and check.

Say the words. Are any of the clusters hard to pronounce?

41 Write sentences using the following words and any others you need. You can only use each word from the box once. Who can use the most words from the box in five minutes?

almost   appalling   are   can   certain   clothes   conditions   couldn't   date   death   from   get   he   I   my   nothing   of   out   over   problem   saved   source   surprise   that   the   there's   trace   was   weather   with   wrong   you   your

42 Using words and phrases from the Word List and Word Plus together with any other language you know, expand the following sentence. How long can you make it?

The young man switched on the computer.

UNIT 11
Pictures and words

→ the past of modal verbs
→ talking about art and writing
→ reacting to stories

Listening: wallpaper

1 **Discussion** Work in pairs. Look at the rooms. Which do you like best? Why?

))) 2 Listen to Track 57. It is an extract from a play called *By Design*.
Two people (Annabelle and Keith) are talking about a friend called George.

What has George just done and what do Annabelle and Keith think about it?

3 **Fact check** Which picture is most like the wallpaper that Annabelle describes?

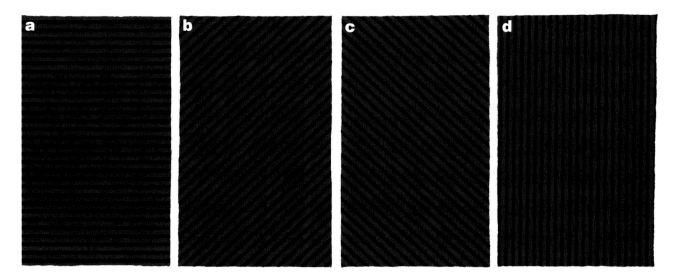

In which picture are the lines *horizontal*? In which are they *diagonal*? In which
are they *vertical*?

4 Complete the extract from Track 57 with one word for each gap.

ANNABELLE: It's got black lines on it, ... lines, you know from the
bottom left to the .... right at about 45 degrees.

KEITH: And you can .... them?

ANNABELLE: See what?

KEITH: ....

ANNABELLE: Why .... you?

KEITH: Because, well, ... on black. They must be ....
– the lines I mean.

ANNABELLE: Well they aren't. The lines are a bit .... than the
background. I .... that was it. Or vice versa.

● ● ● Pronunciation: intonation for reactions and questions

5 Listen to Track 58 and punctuate the end of the lines in the following extracts. You can use full stops, question marks and exclamation marks.

Extract 1
ANNABELLE: ... he's had new wallpaper put in
KEITH: New wallpaper
ANNABELLE: Yes
KEITH: And
ANNABELLE: And, well it's rather special wallpaper
KEITH: In what way
ANNABELLE: Well it's black
KEITH: Black
ANNABELLE: Black
KEITH: Just black
ANNABELLE: Well, not <u>just</u> black

Extract 2
KEITH: Well, I suppose a few hundred, no maybe, let's see, about twelve hundred pounds
ANNABELLE: Uh uh
KEITH: Fifteen hundred
ANNABELLE: Uh uh
KEITH: Two thousand
ANNABELLE: Go on
KEITH: Three thousand? Four thousand
ANNABELLE: More than that
KEITH: Five thousand? Ten thousand
ANNABELLE: Don't stop
KEITH: Fifteen thousand? Twenty thousand
ANNABELLE: Twenty thousand quid
KEITH: That's not possible
ANNABELLE: Oh yes it is
KEITH: For wallpaper
ANNABELLE: For wallpaper
KEITH: Twenty thousand quid For black wallpaper
ANNABELLE: Well, he's always had expensive tastes

6 What helped you to complete Activity 5? Can you say the lines in exactly the same way as the speakers on the Track?

7 How well do you think Annabelle, Keith and George get on?

8 Match the following phrases with the numbers in the pictures.

a at the bottom of the picture
b at the top of the picture
c in the background
d in the bottom, left-hand corner
e in the foreground
f in the middle of the picture
g in the top, right-hand corner
h on the left of the picture
i on the right of the picture

9 **Practice** Student A, turn to Activity Bank 12 on page 155. Student B, turn to Activity Bank 19 on page 158.

10 Match the pictures with the paragraphs. Put the number of the matching picture in the brackets.

a It is a film based on a play called *The Taming of the Shrew* by William Shakespeare. The film is set in an American high school. [   ]

b It is a sculpture by Antony Gormley. It stands by a motorway in the north of England. There was some controversy about it at first but now it is one of the most popular public works of art in Britain. [   ]

c It is a novel by Stephen King that tells the story of a writer. He has an accident and is then kidnapped by a crazy woman who admires his work. She keeps him prisoner and nearly kills him. [   ]

d It is a play by Ray Lawler about migrant workers in Australia. Many people see it as the first great work of Australian theatre. It has been performed all over the world since its premiere in 1957. [   ]

11 Complete the gaps in the table with the words or phrases in blue from Activity 10.

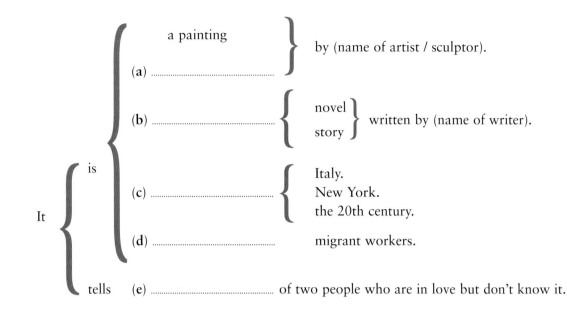

a painting }
(a) .... } by (name of artist / sculptor).

(b) .... { novel } written by (name of writer).
                                          { story }

It { is { (c) .... { Italy.
                                              New York.
                                              the 20th century.

(d) .... migrant workers.

tells (e) .... of two people who are in love but don't know it.

●● ● Using a dictionary: pronunciation, collocation and grammar ·······

12 Look at the dictionary entry for *sculpture* and answer the questions.

a What is the difference between the pronunciation of *sculpture* in British and American English?
b What word often follows *sculpture*?
c In the sentence *I prefer painting to sculpture*, is *sculpture* a countable or an uncountable noun?

sculp·ture /'skʌptʃə $ -ər/ *n* **1** [C,U] an object made out of stone, wood, clay etc by an artist: [+of] *a sculpture of an elephant* | *an exhibition of sculpture* **2** [U] the art of making objects out of stone, wood, clay etc

13 **Team game** Get into two teams. Everyone writes the titles of novels, paintings, sculptures, films and plays on separate pieces of paper.

All the pieces of paper are folded and the two teams swap papers.

A player from Team A picks a piece of paper and describes what is written on it (without revealing the title), saying what it is, who it is by, etc. Team A guesses the title as quickly as possible. The team has one minute to describe and guess as many as possible.

Example:

TEAM PLAYER 1: It's a painting. It's by Leonardo da Vinci.

REST OF TEAM: The Mona Lisa.

TEAM PLAYER 1: Right.

TEAM PLAYER 2: It's a film set at the time of the American Civil War. It's the story of a beautiful woman.

REST OF TEAM: Gone With the Wind?

TEAM PLAYER 2: Yes.

Now a player from Team B picks up titles and describes them to their team. How many can they guess in one minute? Which team guesses the most titles?

14 Write the number of the questions about plays and films in the appropriate rows in the table below.

1 What are the best bits in the film?
2 What kind of play is it?
3 Who wrote it?
4 What part does X play in the film?
5 What's the story of the film?
6 Who directed the film / play?
7 Who are the main characters in the film?
8 Who's in it?

a Plot:	
b Type of play or film:	
c Actors:	
d Characters:	
e Memorable scenes:	
f Writer or director:	

Which of the questions *1–8* can you also ask about books if you use *book* instead of *play* or *film*?

15 Copy the table and complete it by interviewing your partner about a book, play or film they have enjoyed. (Check the vocabulary for types of book, play or film in Activity Bank 6 on page 152.)

Reading: Shakespeare?

16 Discussion Which famous writer from your country do all students learn about at some time during their school career?

17 Read the article and write down the connection between William Shakespeare and the following:

a Stratford-upon-Avon
b Romeo and Juliet
c films
d education
e handwritten manuscripts
f the Earl of Oxford

The great Shakespeare controversy:
who really wrote Romeo and Juliet?

William Shakespeare, England's greatest writer, was responsible for 39 plays and some of the most fantastic poetry ever written. He was born in Stratford-upon-Avon on April 23 1564. Later he went to London where he wrote, and acted in, plays such as Romeo and Juliet, Macbeth, Hamlet and The Tempest. He died in Stratford in 1616, but films are still being made about him and his work 400 years later.

However, some people don't believe that William Shakespeare of Stratford could have written the plays. They say that he wasn't educated well enough to know about all the things mentioned in the plays. Besides, there are no manuscripts in Shakespeare's handwriting, and his name didn't even appear on many of his plays until after his death.

One group of people argues that the plays must have been written by Edward de Vere, the Earl of Oxford. He wasn't allowed to use his own name, because he was an aristocrat, and so he chose 'Shakespeare' as a pseudonym.

18 Fact check Are the following statements *True* (*T*) or *False* (*F*)?

a A man called William Shakespeare came from Stratford-upon-Avon.   [   ]
b The Avon is a river.   [   ]
c William Shakespeare was very well educated. [   ]
d People wrote plays and books (manuscripts) by hand in Shakespeare's day.   [   ]
e The Earl of Oxford was a farm labourer.   [   ]
f A pseudonym is a name a person uses instead of their real name.   [   ]

19 Put the following emails between Luke and Hannah in the correct order. *A* is the first one in the sequence.

E

Ah yes, Hannah, but that's the question. Who was he?
Luke
BTW why don't you have a look at the Shakespeare Oxford Society website? http://www.shakespeare-oxford.com

A

Dear Hannah,
Thanks for your mail.
You ask why I think the Earl of Oxford wrote 'Shakespeare's' plays? Well, to start with William Shakespeare of Stratford was uneducated. He didn't go to university or anything. He never travelled. How could he have known all the history in the plays? For example, how did he know all about Italy, where Romeo and Juliet takes place?
Love
Luke

F

Does it matter if I can't prove anything? You can't either. You keep talking about who Shakespeare must have been – he must have been an aristocrat, he must have been educated, he must have been this, he must have been that. But all that matters to me is who he really was.
Hannah

B

Dear Luke,
No writer put their name on their plays in the 1580s and '90s! It just wasn't the custom. But in the first complete collection of all the plays (published in 1623, after Shakespeare's death) Shakespeare is described as the 'sweet swan of Avon'. The River Avon runs through Stratford-upon-Avon. So he must have been talking about William Shakespeare from Stratford.
OK?
Hannah

G

Hannah,
Self-taught Shakespeare! That just can't have happened! Anyway, how come his name wasn't on any of his plays?
Luke

C

Yes, but the Earl of Oxford had an estate in Bilton – and that had a different River Avon near it. The 'swan of Avon' might have been the swan of BILTON-upon-Avon – in other words, the Earl of Oxford.
What do you have to say about that?
Luke

H

Dear Luke,
OK, so perhaps Shakespeare wasn't educated. But his neighbour in Stratford was John Field, who published books – Shakespeare could have read those books to get information about foreign countries and English history. He might have read those. He was probably self-taught.
Best wishes,
Hannah

D

Oh, come on, Luke! Don't repeat that old Oxford Avon story! The Earl of Oxford sold his estate at Bilton in 1580 – and nobody called Shakespeare the 'swan of Avon' until 1623!
Be logical :-)
Hannah

I

Hi Hannah,
'Logical'! You're joking, surely? You'll never be able to prove that the Avon in the 1623 edition of the plays was the Stratford Avon. It could have been a different river, the River Avon at Bilton – whether the Earl of Oxford sold it or not. Let's face it, you can't prove anything about Shakespeare, can you?
Luke

20 Comprehension Answer the following questions.

a Who was John Field and where did he live?
b Who was described as the 'sweet swan of Avon'?
c How many River Avons do Luke and Hannah talk about? Where are they?
d When was the first complete collection of Shakespeare plays published?
e When did the Earl of Oxford sell his estate at Bilton?

21 Match the words and phrases on the left with the explanations of their use on the right.

a anyway   1 is used to introduce a first point to support an argument
b besides   2 is used to introduce a specific instance of something
c for example   3 is used at the beginning of a sentence to change the subject
d to start with   4 is used to say 'in addition to what has just been said'

Language in chunks

22 How many times does Hannah use the word *matter(s)* in her emails? Write down the examples you find.

23 Look at these phrases. In each case *matter(s)* is a verb, except for one. Which one?

> all that matters   what matters   it doesn't matter   what's the matter?
> it matters a lot   the only thing that matters   nothing else matters

24 Complete the following sentences using phrases with *matter(s)* like those in Activity 23.

a I don't care what you wear. All .... is that you get here on time.

b I don't care whether or not Shakespeare wrote Romeo and Juliet. What .... is the play itself.

c 'I'm sorry I forgot to bring the book.' 'Oh, don't worry. It ....'

d It may not be important to you, but it .... to me.

e My family is the most important part of my life. Nothing ....

f You don't have to like Shakespeare's plays. The .... is that you read at least one!

g You look terrible! What .... ?

Grammar: the past of modals

25 Some people copy the work of famous writers (like Shakespeare) or artists (like Picasso).
For each sentence in the left-hand column write the number of the sentence from the
right-hand column that best explains it.

a Shakespeare can't have written that play. It's not his style. [7]   1 I am sure that he wasn't poor.
b Someone might have used his name. [ ]   2 It is certain that he was.
c Shakespeare must have been a very good playwright. [ ]   3 It is impossible that anyone else did it.
d Picasso couldn't have painted this picture. It's too boring. [ ]   4 It is not possible that he painted it.
e Paula King, the famous woman forger, could have   5 It is possible that someone did.
copied Picasso's style. [ ]   6 It's possible that he did.
f I don't think anyone but Picasso could have painted it! [ ]   7 It's not possible that he did it.
g Shakespeare might have written this play. The words   8 It's possible that she did.
sound like his. [ ]
h Picasso sold a lot of paintings during his life. He must have
been very rich. [ ]

Check your answers by looking at **11A** and **11B** in the Mini-grammar.

26 Rewrite the sentences using an appropriate modal verb. (Refer to **11A** and **11B**
in the Mini-grammar, to help you.) Sometimes more than one answer is possible.

a It is possible that Picasso painted this picture, but I can't be sure.
Picasso could / might have painted this picture.

b He painted the whole picture in two hours? That's just not possible.

c Look at all those paintings in her private gallery. I'm sure she was rich.

d The thieves possibly took the painting during the night.

e He didn't steal the painting because he was abroad when it happened.

f It's possible that someone put the picture in my bag.

27 Practice Read the following stories.

a UFO When driving home one night, Jackie and Rod Samuels saw a bright light coming towards them. The light was so bright that Jackie, who was driving, lost control of the car and they hit a wall. When the police came Rod said, 'It wasn't her fault. We had a close encounter with a UFO.'

b Other lives Mary Crewe says she has lived many times before. She tells stories of her childhood in 12th-century York, in the north of England. She can give details that no one else knows about – apparently – and they turn out to be true.

c Shark! Chris Michaels denies copying someone else's work, but his novel Shark! is very similar to Jaws by Peter Benchley. 'I didn't copy it,' he says, 'I've never read anything by Peter Benchley in my life.'

In groups write sentences saying why you do or don't believe the stories.

Example (story A): *I don't think Jackie and Rod Samuels saw a UFO. The bright light might have been ordinary headlights.*

Read out your sentences. Did the other groups think the same?

Functional language: reacting to things you are told

28 Listen to Track 59 and fill in the missing parts of the conversation.

NANCY: How was the film?

JIM: It was a disaster. Halfway through they stopped it and told us we had to leave.

NANCY: (a) ....

JIM: Well, yes. We all had to go out into the street, even though it was raining.

NANCY: (b) ....

JIM: No, it certainly wasn't. I got soaked. But then, when we were allowed back, they started the film again and offered all of us free tickets to any film for the next month.

NANCY: (c) ....

JIM: I certainly was. Would you like to come to the next film with me?

STARRING SIMON STEPHEN
BOX OFFICE NOW OPEN

29 Complete the following replies with words and phrases from the box.

| been easy   exhausted   hurt yourself   much fun   wonderful |

a You were so lucky! That must have been ....*wonderful*........ .

b After all that effort, you must have been ....

c That can't have .... I don't think I could have done it.

d That was a really crazy thing to do. You might have

....

e That couldn't have been ....

30 Respond to the following stories with replies like those in Activity 29.

a 'And then I saw it. The summit of Mount Everest.'
'*That must have been fantastic!*'

b 'And then suddenly he turned white and fell off his chair – right in front of me!'

c 'When the car ran out of petrol, I had to walk for three miles to the nearest garage.'

d 'We had to get the old piano up the stairs.'

e 'When I woke up the house was on fire.'

f 'I met my favourite actor in the street yesterday.'

g 'Last year I won a ticket for the World Cup final in a raffle.'

h 'When we got home we discovered that someone had stolen our television.'

31 Speaking Work in pairs. Tell your neighbour about the best and worst holiday experiences you have ever had. They should react appropriately to what you say.

Writing: first lines (of novels)

32 What does the first line of a story or a novel have to do? Choose one or more of the following.

- be exciting
- be funny
- be mysterious
- describe a character
- describe a place
- give information

33 Here are some first lines from published novels. Which one makes you want to go on and read the rest of the book?

1 All this happened, more or less.
2 Many years later as he faced the firing squad, Colonel Aureliano Buendia was to remember that distant afternoon when his father took him to discover ice.
3 Polly Alter used to like men, but she didn't trust them any more, or have very much to do with them.
4 The place I like best in this world is the kitchen.
5 There was a death at its beginning as there would be a death again at its end.
6 'You too will marry a boy I choose,' said Mrs Rupa Mehra firmly to her younger daughter.

34 Now read these book descriptions. Match the first lines in Activity 33 with these books which they come from.

a *A Suitable Boy* by Vikram Seth. A huge novel about a young girl's search for love – and a husband. Set in India, it presents a panoramic view of a whole nation, and offers a unique insight into the human heart. [   ]

b *The Horse Whisperer* by Nicholas Evans. After a horrific horse-riding accident a young girl is terribly injured – both physically and mentally. Her horse has also been hurt and the girl's mother takes both girl and horse to an expert for help. A moving tale of love and suffering. [   ]

c *Kitchen* by Banana Yoshimoto. The setting is contemporary Japan, where a pair of young women discover the meaning of life. The writing may be simple, but the words stay in the mind long after the book is closed. [   ]

d *One Hundred Years of Solitude* by Gabriel Garcia Márquez. A classic of 20th-century Latin American literature, this novel charts a century of fantastical happenings in the imaginary South American town of Macondo. [   ]

e *Slaughterhouse 5* by Kurt Vonnegut. One of the most original anti-war novels ever written. Billy Pilgrim, a prisoner of war, witnesses the fire-bombing of Dresden, one of the most destructive acts of the 20th-century. Miraculous, bitter and funny. [   ]

f *The Truth about Lorin Jones* by Alison Lurie. A feminist art historian sets out to rescue the reputation of an artist and to discover the truth about her life. But she finds out more than she expected – especially about herself. [   ]

35 Choose a topic from the box.

> a power cut   looking for water in the desert
> a beauty contest   a disastrous driving test
> a wedding

a Write the first sentence of your story about the topic you have chosen.
b Work in small groups. Look at all your first sentences. Which is the best?
c Using the best first sentence write a complete story in not more than ten sentences.

Review: grammar and functional language

36 Rewrite the expressions in blue, in the following sentences, using either *must have*, *couldn't have* or *might have*.

a CUSTOMS OFFICIAL: I believe you thought that we wouldn't search you.

  You must have thought

b TRAVELLER: What on earth? I'm sure somebody put them in my bag.

c CUSTOMS OFFICIAL: It isn't possible that someone else put them in your bag. You said you packed your bag yourself.

d TRAVELLER: Perhaps someone who works for the airline put them in my bag.

e CUSTOMS OFFICIAL: It's not possible that someone who works here put the diamonds in your bag.

f TRAVELLER: Well, perhaps someone put them in my bag at home and I didn't notice.

g CUSTOMS OFFICIAL: Yes, and possibly it was your fairy godmother! You're under arrest!

37 Put the following lines in order to make a conversation between two singers.

a Hard work. We had to do three encores. [ ]
b How was last night's show? [**1**]
c Great. That must have been a nice feeling. [ ]
d I was. Still am. But the audience loved us. [ ]
e That couldn't have been very pleasant – especially since you got home late. [ ]
f The taxi broke down! That can't have been much fun. [ ]
g Well, no, it wasn't. And then my baby son woke me up at six o'clock this morning. [ ]
h So you see why I'm so tired. And now I have to go back and do the show all over again. [ ]
i Yes. It was great. But then the taxi broke down on the way home. [ ]
j Three? You must have been exhausted. [ ]

38 Work in pairs. Think of an object that has just been found in an archaeological dig. Talk about it to another pair without saying what it is. They have to guess what you are talking about.

Example:

PAIR 1

STUDENT A: *It must have been very beautiful.*

STUDENT B: *Yes, and a queen might have worn it.*

STUDENT A: *But it can't have been very comfortable around the neck.*

PAIR 2

STUDENT C: *Is it a necklace?*

Review: vocabulary

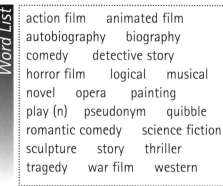

action film   animated film
autobiography   biography
comedy   detective story
horror film   logical   musical
novel   opera   painting
play (n)   pseudonym   quibble
romantic comedy   science fiction
sculpture   story   thriller
tragedy   war film   western

... or vice versa
all that matters is ...
at the bottom / top of the
    (picture)
in the background / foreground
in the bottom / top left- / right-
    hand corner
it doesn't matter
it matters a lot

it's a book / film / play about ...
nothing else matters
on the left / right of the (picture)
the only thing that matters is ...
it's based on
it's set in
to pick a figure at random
what matters is ...
what's the matter?

39 Which words and phrases in the Word List did you know when you started the unit? Tick the words that you knew and draw a circle around the words that were new for you. Choose five of the new words and use them in sentences.

Pronunciation

40 a The letter 'g' can be pronounced in two ways. Find an example of each in the Word List.

Listen to Track 60 and check.

List three other words with each type of 'g' sound.

b Look at the Word List.

1 Write the word with the most syllables and underline the stressed syllable.
2 Write the words with four syllables and underline the stressed syllable for each word.

Listen to Track 61 and check.

41 Work in pairs. Each draw a picture. Include simple objects (e.g. a house, trees, sun / moon, cars, people, buses, dogs, cats). Put your objects in the top and bottom left- and right-hand corners. Don't let your partner see your picture.

Tell your partner what is in your picture. Can they draw the same picture without looking at what you have done?

42 Work in pairs. Design a questionnaire to find out what kinds of entertainment people enjoy (e.g. reading, films, art, theatre). Ask other pairs in the class your questions and write a report on the results.

UNIT 12
Not an easy game

→ conditional sentences
→ injuries (parts of the body)
→ how someone is – e.g. asking how someone is

Speaking: talking about sport

1 **Vocabulary** Name the sports shown in the pictures.

2 **Discussion** In groups, discuss the following questions.

a Which sport is the most dangerous? Which is the least dangerous?
b Have you ever watched or taken part in any of these sports?
c Would you like to? Why / Why not?

3 Complete the first column of the table by yourself. Then ask your partner the questions. Write their answers in the second column.

Which sport:	You	Your partner
... is the most fun to watch?		
... is the least fun to watch?		
... is the one you'd most like to try?		
... is the one you'd least like to try?		
... is the most popular one in your country?		

Listening: football commentary

4 Match the sentence beginnings *a–e* with the correct endings *1–5*. Use a dictionary to help you with words and phrases you do not understand. All the sentences are about the rules of football.

a If the referee gives you a red card
b If you commit a foul
c The place where football is played
d The goalkeeper is the one
e When a player does something against the rules of the game

1 it is called a foul.
2 is called a pitch.
3 the other side gets a free kick.
4 you have to leave the pitch.
5 who tries to stop the ball from going into the net.

5 Listen to Track 62 and answer the questions.

a How many commentators are there?
b Where is the game being played?
c What's the final score?

6 Fact check Listen to Track 62 again. Who:

a ... is given a red card? Miller or Sánchez?
b ... ends up with a broken leg? Miller or Sánchez?
c ... interrupts all the time? Martin or Jim?

7 Look at Track 62 in the Audioscript. Find words in the text with the following meanings. The first letter is given each time.

a the number of goals each team has (s) score
b problems with parts of the body because of accidents (i)
c the left- or right-hand side of the field during a match (w)
d when one player tried to get the ball from another (t)
e the person in control of the match (r)
f the people who try to stop the ball getting into their own goal (d)
g code which says how things must be done in a game (r)

8 Noticing language Listen to Track 62 again. Complete the gaps in these sentences.

a If you kick someone's legs away, you get a ...
b If I was the ... I'd give Miller a red card.
c If they go on playing as well as this they'll ...

Pronunciation:
intonation clues

9 Listen to Track 63. Can you guess the complete football scores? Who won each time?

a Everton 0, Sunderland ...
b Aston Villa 2, Sheffield United ...
c Liverpool 1, Burnley ...
d Newcastle United 2, Manchester United ...
e Blackburn Rovers 0, Sheffield Wednesday ...
f Arsenal 2, Manchester City ...
g Tottenham Hotspur 3, Leeds United ...

Now listen to Track 64 to hear the complete football scores. Were you correct? What helped you decide?

10 Write your own football scores. Read them to a partner using appropriate intonation, but stop just before you give the second score.

Can your partner guess the score?

Example: STUDENT A: Bradford City 3, Leeds ...

STUDENT B: Nil?

STUDENT A: Yes, that's right.

11 Rewrite the following sentence so that it reflects your opinion.

Everyone should support a football team.

Discuss your opinions with the rest of the class.

Grammar: conditionals (*if* sentences)

12 Look at **12A–12D** in the Mini-grammar. Work in pairs and decide what is the difference (if any) between the following pairs of sentences.

a If I were you, I'd be quiet.
   If I was you, I'd be quiet.
b If I went on that television quiz show, I'd win a million pounds.
   If I go on that television quiz show, I'll win a million pounds.
c If she plays well, she'll get a place on the team.
   If she played well, she'd get a place on the team.
d She'll get a place on the team if she plays well.
   If she plays well, she'll get a place on the team.
e If you train properly, you get fit.
   If you trained properly, you'd get fit.

13 In pairs use one of the *if* patterns in **12B–12D** in the Mini-grammar to make sentences for the following situations.

a Someone is upset because their friend has been ignoring them. Give them some advice.

b Someone wants information about different ways of travelling from their village to the capital city. Describe the different possibilities.

c A colleague keeps borrowing your things, and you're really angry about it. You feel you need to confront him. Talk to your colleague about the situation.

d Someone you know is spending all their time going to parties, staying up late and hardly sleeping at all. You think it is starting to affect their work. Give them some advice.

14 Read the following sentences. Are they more like first or second conditional sentences?

a If you are planning to come over tonight, please let me know.
b If you've spoken to him already, I'm going to speak to him tomorrow.
c If you are going to play your guitar, do it quietly.
d If you've finished, put your paper on the table and leave quietly.
e If she gets the job, I'm leaving.
f If she doesn't get the job, a lot of people are going to be very angry.

Say what has replaced the present simple and *will* in each case. Look at 12A and 12C in the Mini-grammar.

Example: In sentence 'a' the present continuous ('you are planning') has replaced the present simple, and an imperative ('let me know') has replaced the 'will' clause.

15 Practice Complete the following sentences.

a If I won a lot of money on the lottery,

....

b If your frying pan catches fire,

....

c If you don't stop talking,

....

d I wouldn't drive as fast as that

....

e If you've never learned to play a musical instrument, ...

f ....
   I'm going to enjoy myself a lot.

g If you're going to say things like that,

....

Reading: the manager

16 Read the text below. Where do you think the text comes from? Is it from:

a ... *Football Manager* (a magazine for anyone interested in running a football club)?
b ... the sports pages of a newspaper?
c ... a novel called *The Manager's Dilemma*?
d ... *Management Today* (a magazine for business people)?

THE MANAGER'S OFFICE

When Paul walked into the manager's office he knew something was wrong. Bob didn't say hello in the usual way. He didn't even look up from his desk. Paul stood there awkwardly wondering whether to shut the door.

Two minutes passed.

'Bob,' he said nervously, 'is something the matter?'

'You tell me,' he replied, looking at him intently, with no trace of a smile. He realised that he was angry about something.

'Look,' he stammered, '(1) .... Or do you want me to just stand here?'

Bob took off his glasses and stood up. He stretched, turned his back on the other man and walked to the large plate-glass window at one side of the room.

'(2) .... ,' he said, so quietly that Paul could hardly hear his voice.

'What do you mean?' He hadn't expected this. 'I am "in shape" as you call it.'

'Are you? Are you really? I don't think so. You've been missing training sessions, and I think you're unfit and – on top of that –' Bob picked up that morning's newspaper, 'I have to read about you in the *Daily Mirror*. Look at this!' he almost shouted at him, 'What on earth were you thinking of?'

'(3) ....'

'There's nothing to explain, Paul. You're out every evening at fashionable parties having a good time with your friends. God knows what you get up to. I've had enough of it.' He turned to face him. 'Frankly, Paul, I think I've had enough of you.'

'(4) ....'

'You'd what, Paul? Leave the club? Complain to the manager? But that's just the problem for you isn't it? I am the manager.'

'Look, Bob, I'm sorry; honestly I am.' He walked over to stand beside him. From here you could see right into the stadium. Some of his team-mates were down there kicking balls around. He should be with them. He knew that. But he'd got up late and he felt terrible.

'(5) ....' There. He had said it.

'You can't mean that.'

'Oh but I do, Paul, I do. Just because we have the same mother and father ... .'

'Brothers Bob! We're brothers. Go on, say it, I know it's difficult for you. You've always hated the fact that I'm a great footballer, better than you could ever be. Sometimes I wonder how we can exist in the same club ... .'

'That makes two of us, Paul.'

The silence in the room grew louder. Paul didn't know what to say or do. It was true that he had missed a lot of training sessions. It was true he was going out a lot. But that's because everyone asked him to. He was one of the most famous players in the world. The newspapers wanted photographs of him all the time. People wanted to talk to him. They wanted to get to know him. Anyway, he enjoyed going out, he liked the attention. As for the team, the club ... .

'So tell me,' Bob said, interrupting his thoughts, 'how important is the game to you? How much do you want to play?'

Paul's brother must have read his thoughts. What could he say to him now?

17 Read the following lines of conversation. They have been taken out of the text on page 122. Find the right place (*1–5*) for each in the text.

a If I thought you meant that, I'd … [ ]
b If I've done anything to offend you, anything at all, please tell me. [ ]
c If you don't change your ways, you'll be out of the team. [ ]
d If you don't get in shape soon, I'll have to let you go. [ ]
e If you'd just let me explain … [ ]

18 Answer the following questions.

a Who is the player?
b Who is the manager?
c What is the game?
d Why is the manager angry with the player? Give three reasons.
e What is the relationship between the manager and the player?

19 Vocabulary Find words or phrases in the text with the following meanings. The first letter of each word is given.

a with a feeling of embarrassment, not knowing what to say (a)
b to speak with pauses and repeated sounds because you are nervous (s)
c to straighten your arms, back, etc. for relaxation (s)
d almost not (h)
e times when teams practise to get fit (two words) (t, s)
f popular at a particular time (f)
g to do something a little bit bad or wicked (three words) (g, u, t, something)
h a large building for football matches, with a pitch and seats (s)

Language in chunks

20 Complete the following phrases with words from the text. The meanings are given in brackets.

a he ....*turned his back*.... on the other man (he turned round, away from him)
b if you don't .... soon (become fit)
c I've .... you (it has been too much for me)
d if you don't .... (behave differently)
e That................................. (I feel exactly the same as you)
f .... his thoughts (stopping him thinking)
g he must have .... (guessed what he was thinking)

21 Choose two of the phrases and use them in sentences of your own.

Vocabulary: parts of the body; injuries

22 Look at the picture. Put the words below with the right boxes.

ankle	stomach
collar bone	throat
ear	thumb
elbow	toes
eye	tooth
index finger	waist
little finger	wrist
heel	big toe
knee	thigh
nose	

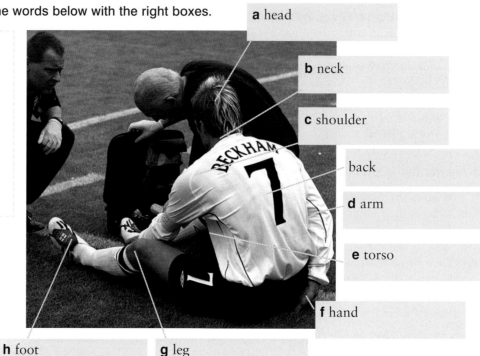

a head

b neck

c shoulder

back

d arm

e torso

f hand

h foot   **g** leg

23 What is the footballer's problem, do you think?

●●● Using a dictionary: how a word is used

24 Look at the dictionary entry for *swollen*.

a What part of speech is it?
b What can it be used to describe, apart from parts of the body?
c What is special about someone with a *swollen head*?

swollen¹ /ˈswəʊlən/ adj ★
1 an area of your body that is swollen has increased in size as a result of an injury or illness: *a swollen hand/ knee/foot*
2 a swollen river or stream contains more water than normal as a result of heavy rain or snow that has MELTED
have a swollen head to think that you are more clever, important etc than you really are because you have been successful at something
sw̲…l̲en² the past participle of swell¹

25 Copy and complete the tables using the words from Activity 22.

earache,	+ ache

Note: with *stomach* and *tummy* (= an informal word for *stomach*) we use hyphens (*stomach-ache*, *tummy-ache*). With other words we make one word (e.g. *earache*).

1 broken	*broken ankle,*
2 fractured	
3 sprained	
4 swollen	
5 sore	
6 a pain in the ...	

26 Play a mime game. Get into two teams. A player from one team mimes an illness or an injury. Their team has to guess what it is. Then it is the other team's turn.

27 Speaking Have you ever broken, fractured or sprained something? Tell your partner about it.

Functional language: asking how someone is

28 Before you listen to Track 65, put Jane's questions and answers in the right gaps.

VICKY: Hi, Jane, how are you?

JANE: (**a**) ....

VICKY: Oh, fine, I suppose. You're looking well, by the way.

JANE: (**b**) ....

VICKY: Good.

JANE: (**c**) ....

VICKY: Thanks!

JANE: (**d**) ....

VICKY: It's all right. It's true; I have been a bit under the weather recently, – work, that kind of thing.

JANE: (**e**) ....

VICKY: Oh, I don't really think I'm up to it. Do you mind?

JANE: (**f**) ....

Now listen to Track 65. Were you correct?

1 But what about you? You look terrible.
2 I'm fine. How about you?
3 No sorry, I mean …
4 Oh, poor you. Listen, why not come round after the practice and I'll try and cheer you up.
5 No, not at all. Get well soon.
6 Thanks. I had an infection. I was off work, but I'm better now.

29 Copy and complete the table with language from the conversation in Activity 28.

a Asking how someone is, or commenting on how they look:
b Saying how you are or how you have been:
c Reacting to how someone is:

Where would you put the following in the table above?

1 I'm fine (now).
2 How awful.
3 I've broken my leg.
4 I heard you'd been ill / in an accident.
5 I've sprained my ankle.
6 I was in an accident.
7 I'm not very well, actually.
8 I've been ill.
9 I've got …
10 Oh, I'm pleased to hear that.
11 That's great.
12 What happened to you?
13 Oh, I'm sorry to hear that.

30 Which of the following describe a specific illness or problem? Which describe the way you feel? Put the following words and phrases into the correct box (*a* or *b*) below.

a bad back   ill   flu   a migraine   sick
a stomach-ache   food poisoning   terrible
a cold   not very well   off-colour

a to have (a specific illness / problem):
b to feel:

31 Work in pairs. Choose one of the following situations and make up a conversation between the people. Act it out for the rest of the class.

a Two friends meet after one of them has been in hospital because of a bad chest infection, but is better now.
b Two colleagues meet at work. One of them is feeling really ill and is about to go home and go to bed.
c Two friends meet. One of them has their leg in plaster.

32 Read the article. Match the pictures *1–4* with the paragraphs.

Dealing with a sports injury

If you hurt yourself, stop immediately. If the injury seems minor, follow the **RICE** principles.

R is for Rest. Give painful muscles plenty of time to recover if you want to avoid serious damage. If it hurts, avoid exercise until you can gently begin again. If the injury is less serious, you can do 'active rest', which means gently exercising the area until it is back to its former strength and full range of movement. Pain is the guide – if it really hurts, seek medical attention. [   ]

I is for Ice. Apply using an ice pack or even a bag of frozen peas wrapped in a towel. Keep it on the sprain or strain for 15 minutes and repeat several times in the first 48 hours. If the swelling and pain do not disappear, seek medical help. Don't apply heat, because this increases the blood circulation and swelling in damaged areas. [   ]

C is for Compress. A bandage or elastic support worn over the injury will help stop bleeding and reduce the swelling. But it won't work if the compress is too tight or too loose. [   ]

E is for Elevate. If it is a minor injury (particularly in the case of the knee, foot or ankle), resting and raising the leg by more than 20 or 30 degrees above hip level within 24 hours of the injury will prevent or reduce swelling. [   ]

NB: **RICE** is a recognised acronym used by chartered physiotherapists in the UK.

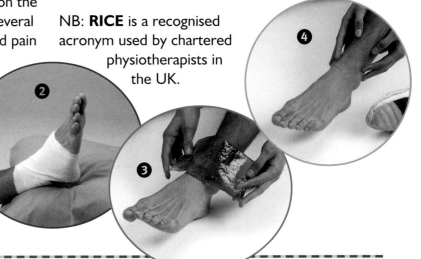

33 Explain the importance of the following in the RICE principles.

a pain
b a bag of frozen peas
c a towel
d heat
e a bandage
f hip level

34 Look at the following dictionary definition of acronym.

acronym: a word made up of the first letters of other words

a Join phrases from the two columns to make names. What are the acronyms?

Self-Contained	by Stimulated Emission of Radiation
Light Amplification	Educational Scientific and Cultural Organisation
North Atlantic	Tax
United Nations	Treaty Organisation
Value Added	Underwater Breathing Apparatus

b Can you think of acronyms in your language? Explain them to the rest of the class.

35 Writing Make up an acronym to help people to remember what to do in a particular situation. Describe what each letter in your acronym stands for. You can choose one of the following situations or invent one of your own.

- Having people for dinner
- Using a technical device (e.g. a computer program, a mobile phone)
- Planning a journey / holiday
- Preparing for an exam
- Having a party

Example:

Having people for dinner

> *Meet … your guests with a smile on your face.*
>
> *Entertain … your guests and make sure they talk to each other.*
>
> *Agreement … is better than argument around the dinner table.*
>
> *Leave … the washing-up until afterwards.*

Review: grammar and functional language

36 Complete the dialogue with one word in each gap.

MAN: Taxi! Taxi!
DRIVER: Where would you like to go, sir?
MAN: Harrington Square, please.
DRIVER: Right you are, sir. There's a lot of traffic today. Do you think it (**a**) .... be quicker if I went through Austin Street?
MAN: Not sure about that. If I (**b**) .... you, I think I'd go round by the park.
DRIVER: Too late for that now. I don't think that's a good idea, sir. If I (**c**) .... that way, I always get stuck at the roundabout.
MAN: OK, yes, you're right. It's my fault anyway. If I (**d**) .... my journey earlier, I wouldn't always be late.
DRIVER: You're not to blame, sir. If this taxi only went a bit faster we (**e**) .... be halfway there
MAN: Watch out!
DRIVER: Phew! That was close!
MAN: Yes, it certainly was. If you always (**f**) .... that fast, you're (**g**) .... to knock a cyclist down one of these days! How about driving just a bit more slowly!
DRIVER: Sorry sir. But if cyclists (**h**) .... take so many risks they wouldn't have so many accidents. Anyway I'd better hurry – otherwise you won't get to Harrington Square on time.
MAN: Actually, I think I'd prefer to be late!
DRIVER: That's your decision, sir, but if you (**i**) .... not worried about the time …
MAN: Yes, what?
DRIVER: Well, I mean, why did you ask me to get there as fast as possible?
MAN: I didn't.
DRIVER: Didn't you?

37 Match the sentences on the left with the replies on the right.

a	How are you?	1	I broke my leg in a football game.
b	I've got a terrible cold.	2	Fine. How are you?
c	I'm feeling much better these days.	3	Oh, I am pleased to hear that.
d	I heard you'd been ill.	4	Poor you.
e	What happened to you?	5	Thanks. I'm feeling fine.
f	You look terrible.	6	Well yes, I'm not feeling too great.
g	You're looking well.	7	Yes, but I'm better now.

38 Complete the following sentences as if you are the person in brackets.

a (Teacher explaining the rules of tennis) If your ball goes into the net ...

b (Referee to football player) If you do that again ...

c (Friend advising a boxer who doesn't enjoy boxing) If I were you ...

d (Football team manager talking to club owner) If he put a bit more effort into his training sessions ...

e (Tennis player talking to opponent) If the rain goes on like this ...

f (Friend explaining the rules of a board game) If you land on this square ...

Write your own rules for a game. Write two rules which are correct and two which are incorrect. Work in pairs. Can your partner guess which rules are incorrect?

Review: vocabulary

acronym   American football   ankle   arm   awkwardly
back   big toe   boxing   break   collar bone   defender
diving   ear   elbow   eye   fashionable   foot   football
fractured   hand   hardly   head   horse-riding   index finger
injury   judo   leg   neck   referee   rule   score   shoulder
sore   sprained   stadium   stiff   stomach-ache   swollen
thigh   stammer   stretch   tackle   torso   training session
waist   wing   wrist

a pain in the (back)
that makes two of us
to be an item
to change (your) ways
to get into shape
to get up to
to have enough of something
to interrupt somebody's thoughts
to read somebody's thoughts
to turn (your) back on somebody

39 Look at the following 'wordmap'. Extend it by adding more balloons and more words. See how far you can extend it.

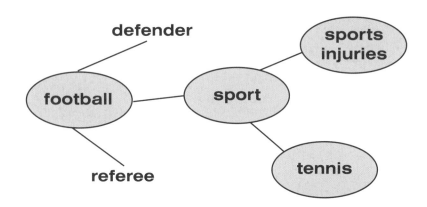

● ● ● Pronunciation

40 Which is the odd one out in the following groups?

a flu   rule   toe   tooth   two

b broken   cold   swollen   throat   tooth

Listen to Track 66 and check.

41 Try to make a new word from the following words by changing only one sound.

a ankle *uncle*
b thumb
c pain
d hand
e nose
f wrist
g sore

42 Game Team A names a part of the body. Team B has to combine it with as many words from the Word List as possible. Score one point for each word, and lose one point for each mistake.

Example: TEAM A: *stomach*

TEAM B: *stomach-ache, a pain in my stomach, a sore stomach, a broken stomach*

(TEAM B would only get two points because we don't say a broken stomach.)

43 Writing Which of the following words go together?

child   husband   manager   parent
student   teacher   wife   worker

Example: *child – parent*

Work in pairs. Choose one pair of words and write a short dialogue between the two people. One of them has a problem and the other tries to help. Use as many phrases from Word Plus as you can. Act out your scene for the rest of the class.

Reading: a special concert

1   Read the text and answer the questions which follow.

THE CONCERT

There was only one chair on the stage of the concert hall in northern England. There was no piano, no music stand and no conductor. Just that solitary chair.

The atmosphere in the hall was tense. People were nervous and excited. Everyone in the audience of 600 people knew that they were going to hear a very special kind of music.

Finally it was time to start. Yo-Yo Ma, one of the world's most famous cellists, came on to the stage, bowed to the audience and sat down quietly on the chair. He made himself comfortable, thought for some minutes until there was complete silence, and then he started to play music that was at first empty and dangerous, but that soon became loud and painful, like the worst thing you've ever heard. It was almost unbearable but then, finally, it faded away to nothing. Yo-Yo Ma did not move. He stayed with his head bowed over his instrument.

Everyone in the hall held their breath. For what seemed like hours, nobody moved. It was as if they had all experienced something terrible and dark.

But then Yo-Yo Ma stood up. He put down his cello. He stretched out his hand to someone in the audience, asking them to come and join him. An electric shock ran through the audience when they realised what was going to happen.

A man got up from his seat and walked towards the stage. He was dressed in dirty motorcycle leathers, but Ma did not seem to mind. He rushed down from the stage, and when the two men met they flung their arms around each other in an emotional embrace.

The audience went crazy; suddenly everyone was cheering and shouting, like people do when they've just heard great music. But this was more than music.

a Who played at the concert?
b How many people were in the audience?
c What was the music like?
d How did the audience react as the music finished?
e What happened next?
f How did the audience react then?

2 Work in groups of three. Why does the text say 'This was more than music'? What do you think is the connection between the music, Yo-Yo Ma and the man dressed in motorcycle leathers? To find out:

STUDENT A: look at Activity Bank 13 on page 155.
STUDENT B: look at Activity Bank 20 on page 158.
STUDENT C: look at Activity Bank 22 on page 159.

3 Now answer the following questions.

a What was the piece of music in the concert called?
b Who wrote it?
c Why did he write it?
d What had Vedran Smailovic done and why?
e Who was the man in the audience wearing motorcycle leathers?

Language in chunks

4 Explain the meaning of the phrases in blue from the reading texts.

a He made himself comfortable.
b There was complete silence.
c Everyone held their breath.
d They flung their arms around each other.
e The audience went crazy.

5 Use the phrases from Activity 4 to answer the following questions. You may have to change the tense of the verb and some other words.

a What do you do when you swim underwater?
b What do you do at the start of a long rail journey?
c What might you hear in the middle of the Arctic or Antarctic?
d What would you and your best friend do if you met after not seeing each other for a long time?
e What would you do at the end of a concert by your favourite musician?

6 What words would you choose from the following to describe Vedran Smailovic's action? What other words could you use?

| beautiful | brave | crazy | dramatic |
| foolish | gentle | irresponsible | useless |

Vocabulary: hobbies and professions (word formation)

7 Match the words with the numbers in the pictures.

a	bass guitar	[6]	g	piano	[ ]
b	cello	[ ]	h	saxophone	[ ]
c	double bass	[ ]	i	trombone	[ ]
d	drums	[ ]	j	trumpet	[ ]
e	guitar	[ ]	k	violin	[ ]
f	keyboard	[ ]			

8 Look at the way we make words to describe what people do by using suffixes or adding words, and then do the activity below.

●●● WORDS FOR PROFESSIONS AND ACTIVITIES

1 To make words that describe what people do, we often add the suffix *-ist* to the noun:
guitar→guitarist   cello→cellist   bass→bassist   science→scientist
But after a verb that describes the activity we add the suffix *-er*, or sometimes *-or*:
run→runner   act→actor   drum→drummer

---

2 People who play sports or games are often called *players*:
tennis→tennis player   badminton→badminton player
Musicians can also be called *players*, especially if the instrument they play has two or more syllables:
keyboard→keyboard player   harpsichord→harpsichord player

---

3 Some important exceptions are:
football→footballer   athletics→athlete   mathematics→mathematician   cooking→cook   yacht→yachtsman

---

What is the word for someone who:

a ... composes music? ....

b ... manages a band? ....

c ... sings? ....

d ... plays the cello? ....

e ... plays football? ....

f ... plays chess? ....

g ... takes photographs? ....

h ... teaches? ....

i ... works at reception in a hotel? ....

●●● Pronunciation: stressed syllables

9 Underline the stressed syllable in each of the following words.

   a mathematics
   b photograph
   c piano
   d saxophone
   e biology
   f therapy
   g trombone
   h violin
   i reception
   j journal

10 Listen to the words on Track 67 and copy them down. Underline the stressed syllable. Notice how sometimes the stress is different from the related word in Activity 9. Is the *Same* syllable (*S*) or a *Different* syllable (*D*) stressed?

Example: *mathematician – D*

---

11 Use some of the words from Activities 8–10 to identify the occupations in the pictures.

a ....

b ....

c ....

d ....

e ....

f ....

g ....

h ....

i ....

j ....

k ....

12 Speaking Which of these jobs would you most like to do? Why? Tell your partner your reasons.

Speaking: talking about music

13 Think of a piece of music you really like and complete the first column.

	You	Your partner
What type of music is it? (e.g. classical, jazz, pop, folk, dance)		
How would you describe it to a friend?		
What 'colour' is it?		
What's the mood of the music?		
Where would you most like to hear it?		

14 Interview your partner and complete the second column with what they have to say.

15 Tell the rest of the class about what your partner said. Has anyone chosen the same piece of music?

Grammar: verb patterns

16 Look at **13A** in the Mini-grammar. Which is the correct sentence in each pair? Circle *1* or *2*.

  a 1 Isla enjoys to listen to jazz.
      2 Isla enjoys listening to jazz.
  b 1 She offered to buy her friend a ticket to a jazz concert.
      2 She offered buying her friend a ticket to a jazz concert.
  c 1 He agreed to go with her.
      2 He agreed going with her.
  d 1 She suggested to meet at seven o'clock.
      2 She suggested meeting at seven o'clock.
  e 1 He promised arriving on time.
      2 He promised to arrive on time.
  f 1 Isla expected to see him outside the jazz club.
      2 Isla expected seeing him outside the jazz club.
  g 1 The next day he denied forgetting about their arrangement!
      2 The next day he denied to forget about their arrangement!

17 What exactly do the following sentences mean?

  a She stopped to tie her shoelaces.

She stopped what she was doing and tied her shoelaces.

  b She remembered meeting him at a concert.
  c Keith forgot sending that letter to his friend.
  d I stopped running and had a rest.
  e I hope you remember to phone me.
  f Julie forgot to water the plants.
  g We never stop talking, you and I!

18 Copy and complete the following sentences with phrases which include an *-ing* form, *to* + infinitive, or *that* + clause. (Use **13A** and **13B** in the Mini-grammar to help you.)

  a I asked my mother for advice and she suggested …
  b My best friend enjoys …
  c When the police questioned him, he denied …
  d I'll come in a minute. I haven't finished …
  e I'm sorry I'm late. I stopped …
  f She promised …
  g When they met she agreed …
  h Michael suddenly realised that he had always disliked …
  i After a lot of discussion they decided …

19 **Game** Get into two teams and follow the instructions. You will need two sets of blank cards.

  a Write the verbs from Mini-grammar 13A and 13B on one set of cards.
  b Write nouns from this unit on another set of cards.
  c Put the cards face down in two piles: one for verbs, one for nouns.
  d A player from Team A picks up one card from each pile and has to make a sentence using the verb and the noun. They get two points for a correct answer, but lose one point if they make mistakes with the verb or the noun.
  e Now a player from Team B picks up a card from each pile and has to make a sentence to try and score two points.

Listening: which Susan?

20 Discussion What would you expect to do if you had to do the following tests? Write notes.

a an audition for a music group or an orchestra
b an audition for a play
c an interview for a new job
d a trial for a place on a sports team
e a language oral exam

21 Read the information about the following people. Listen to Track 68 and say which one of the three people you think is talking.

Susan Bakewell is a hospital nurse who works with children. In her spare time she plays the double bass. She has to audition to get into a local orchestra.

Susan Blewitt is an immigration officer. When she is not working, Susan paints pictures of the countryside, and studies Russian. She has a Russian oral exam coming up.

Susan Shellworth is a lawyer, but away from work she spends all her time training at her local athletics track. She's hoping to compete in the next Olympic Games.

Using a dictionary: how words combine and change

22 Look at the entries for *tune* and answer the questions.

a What other words can you think of which mean *tune*?
b How many phrases does *tune* occur in?
c How many of the phrases are about music? How many refer to something else?

tune¹ /tjuːn/ noun [C] *informal* ★★ a song or piece of music: *a Russian folk tune* ♦ *the station that plays all your favourite tunes*
be in/out of tune with 1 to understand/not understand the feelings, opinions, or needs of a group of people: *He was in tune with current political issues.* **2** to be/not be similar to something and combine well/not combine well with it: *The peaceful setting was in tune with his mood.* **3** to agree/not agree with someone: *We are not in tune with their economic policies.*
call the tune *informal* to be in control of something
change your tune or **sing a different tune** *informal* to change your opinion or attitude
dance to sb's tune *informal* to do what someone tells you to do
in/out of tune producing the right/wrong note when you sing or play music: *One of the guitars sounds a little out of tune.*
to the tune of used for emphasizing how large an amount is: *The company is in debt to the tune of £1.2 billion.*

23 Listen to Track 69 and answer the questions.

    a Which of the five tests in Activity 20 was the speaker involved in?

    b Was she successful or not?

    c What did the speaker think of the experience?

24 Match the words and phrases from Track 69 with their definitions.

a accompanist	**1** a quick rehearsal of a piece of music
b in tune	**2** a series of notes going up and down with fixed intervals between them
c run-through	**3** playing the music straightaway, the first time you see it
d scale	**4** usually a pianist who plays along with the solo player
e sight-reading	**5** when the notes sound right, rather than ugly, because they are not too high or too low

25 Fact check Listen to Track 69 again and answer the questions.

    a What three things did the speaker have to do in the audition?

    b How many people were in the room?

    c What day was the audition?

    d What day was the next orchestra practice?

    e Who did the speaker phone to talk about the audition?

    f When did the speaker know if she had been successful?

26 Find the following phrases (in blue) in Track 69 in the Audioscript and match them to the meanings (*a–f*).

What on earth (am I doing here)?   I may as well (go home).
(I may as well) see it through.   I can be out of here.
(I sort of breathed) a huge sigh of relief.   Do I take that as (a 'yes')?

    a a large exhalation of breath because something is finished

    b continue until the end

    c I can leave

    d it would be a good idea to

    e Do I understand that to be …

    f what (*made stronger*)

Functional language: showing concern

27 Put the following lines of a conversation in the right order.

[1] How was the exam?
[   ] You didn't have to do it!
[   ] It was terrible.
[   ] Oh, come on! I'm sure it wasn't that bad.
[   ] Why? What happened?
[   ] I couldn't answer one of the questions.
      I made a real mess of it.

Now listen to Track 70. Were you correct?

28 Put the expressions in the right place (a–i) on the scale. The first
    one has been done for you.

100% (very good)

Absolutely terrible.	a	....
It was great.	b	....
I couldn't think what to say / write.	c	....
It wasn't too bad.	d	....
I think it went OK.	e	....
It could have been worse.	f	....
Horrible.	g	....
It went really well.	h	....
I made a real mess of it.	i	*Absolutely terrible.*

0% (very bad)

29 Are the following sentences responding to *Good News* (GN)
    or *Bad News* (BN)?

a I bet you did all right, really.   [   ]
b I'm really pleased to hear it.   [   ]
c I'm sure it wasn't as bad as all that.   [   ]
d I'm sure it wasn't as bad as you think it was.   [   ]
e It can't have been that bad.   [   ]
f Oh, you poor thing.   [   ]
g Oh good.   [   ]
h That's great.   [   ]
i That sounds terrible.   [   ]

30 Give each of the following a score from *0* (= *I don't / wouldn't mind
    this at all.*) to *5* (= *Just the thought of it completely terrifies me!*).

Activity	Score
doing an audition (music, dance or acting)	
being interviewed on the radio	
doing a driving test	
doing an exam	
going for a job interview	
having an annual review of your progress with your boss / head of department / principal	
meeting your girlfriend's / boyfriend's family for the first time	
visiting the dentist	
something else (*say what*) ...	

Compare your scores with a partner's.

31 Choose two of your partner's
    items from Activity 30 with the
    highest and lowest scores.
    Role-play a conversation as if the
    experience has just happened.

Example:

STUDENT A: *Where have you been?*

STUDENT B: *I've just been
           interviewed on the
           radio.*

STUDENT A: *How was it?*

STUDENT B: *Absolutely terrifying.
           The most frightening
           thing I've ever done.*

STUDENT A: *Oh come on. I'm sure
           it wasn't as bad as
           all that ...*

Writing: for and against

32 **Discussion** Work in small groups. Are tests and exams the best way to measure knowledge? What are their advantages and disadvantages?

33 Look at these three examples of note-taking. In each case the student is preparing for an essay on the topic of exams. Which example do you prefer and why?

A Point by point

Exams

1 efficient
    a everyone takes them at the same time
    b easy to administer
    c easy to mark
2 motivating
    a students have a goal
    b good fun

B Spidergram

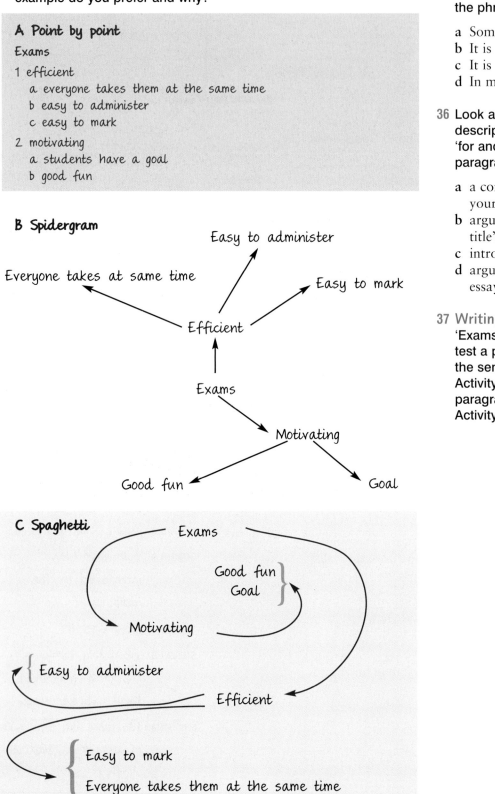

C Spaghetti

34 Make your own notes in preparation for an essay with the title 'Exams are not the best way to test a person's knowledge'.

35 Using your notes from Activity 34, make sentences starting with the phrases below.

    a Some people think that …
    b It is said that …
    c It is (not) true to say that …
    d In my opinion …

36 Look at the following descriptions of paragraphs in a 'for and against' essay. Put the paragraphs in the correct order.

    a a concluding paragraph giving your own opinion
    b arguments against the essay title's point of view
    c introductory paragraph
    d arguments in favour of the essay title's point of view

37 **Writing** Write an essay entitled 'Exams are not the best way to test a person's knowledge'. Use the sentences you wrote in Activity 35 and follow the paragraph order you chose in Activity 36.

Review: grammar and functional language

38 Write the correct word or words in the gaps, using the words in the brackets.

When the policeman arrested Ruth in the supermarket and took her to the police station, she admitted (**a** she / have) ....*that she had*.... some things in her bag which she had not paid for, but she denied (**b** she / take) .... them. She began (**c** offer) .... to pay for the things straightaway so that she could take her six-year-old daughter Jane home, but the policeman told her to stop (**d** talk) ...., and said that he intended (**e** take) .... action over the incident.

At that moment, Jane started (**f** cry) .... When the police officer asked what the matter was, Ruth said that her daughter hated (**g** listen) .... to their conversation. The officer said that he did not like (**h** be) .... unkind, but he could not ignore a crime like this. But he agreed to stop (**i** ask) .... questions until Jane was happier.

When Jane finally stopped (**j** cry) ...., she told them that she had put the things in her mother's bag. Jane didn't realise that her mother would get into trouble. In the end the police officer decided (**k** he / believe) .... Jane. He agreed (**l** he / be) .... a little unkind, but he suggested (**m** Ruth / watch) .... her daughter a bit more carefully. Ruth promised (**n** she / do) .... that and left the police station a sadder but wiser person.

39 Write sentences using the verbs in the box. Follow the verbs with as many verb patterns as possible.

admit	agree	avoid	decide	deny	dislike	enjoy
expect	finish	forget	like	offer	promise	remember
start	stop	suggest	want			

Example: *agree: He agreed to see her at eight.*

He agreed that he would see her at eight.

40 Work in pairs. Ask your partner how they got on in an exam, interview, audition or sports trial. Choose either an appropriate answer or an inappropriate one. Your partner has to say which it was.

Example: STUDENT A: *How did you get on in your trial?*

STUDENT B: *I made a real mess of it.*

STUDENT A: *I'm really pleased to hear it.*

STUDENT B: *That's inappropriate.*

Review: vocabulary

Word List

accompanist   actor   admit   athlete
audience   audition   avoid   bass guitar
cello   composer   concert   conductor
decide   deny   double bass   drums   enjoy
exam   expect   finish   flute   forget
guitar   in tune   interview   keyboard
manager   offer   oral exam   percussion
photographer   piano   receptionist
remember   run-through   saxophone   scale
sight reading   singer   songwriter
sports trial   suggest   therapist   trombone
trumpet   tune   violin

Word Plus

I may as well (go home now).
can I take that as a
   'yes' / 'no'?
it could have been worse
to be constantly under attack
to be in tune
to be out of here
to breathe a (huge) sigh of
   relief
to do something about it

to fling your arms around
   someone
to go crazy
to hold (your) breath
to make a real mess of
   something
to make yourself
   comfortable
to see something through

41 Which of the words and expressions in the Word List do you think will be most useful for you in the future? Why? Which do you think will be the least useful?

Pronunciation

42 What common sound do the words in each group below (a–c) share: /aɪ/ like *light*, /iː/ like *see*, or /ɪ/ like *sit*?

a audition, badminton, exam, guitar, trumpet, violin ....

b athlete, keyboard, pianist ....

c might, right, trial, violin, writer ....

Listen to Track 71 and check.

43 Look at the following words and mark the stress patterns.

a receptionist   b percussion
c saxophone   d violin

Listen to Track 72 and check.

44 Listen to Track 73. Write the words you hear in the correct column. The circles indicate the number of syllables and the large circle shows the stressed syllable.

a Ooo	b oOo	c ooO	d oOoo
audience			

Write two more words that you can think of that have the same stress pattern in each column in the table.

45 Game Team A chooses any two words from the Word List. Team B has to use them both in one sentence.

Example:

TEAM A: 'Bass guitar' and 'write'.

TEAM B: After she had chosen a bass guitar, she wrote a cheque to pay for it.

46 Work in groups of five. Each student should write the following sentence at the top of a piece of paper.

'What on earth am I doing here?' she thought as she walked into the room.

Write the next sentence to continue the story. Then pass your paper to the student on your left and write the next sentence of the story that you receive.

Repeat this five times until you have your own piece of paper back again.

Write the final sentence.

Read out the five stories. Choose the best and read it to the rest of the class.

UNIT 14
Getting along

→ direct and indirect speech
→ friends and enemies
→ invitations

Listening: he had a nice smile (mini-narratives)

1 Before you listen to the people talking, look at the pictures, and at the speakers' opening words. What do you think is going to happen in each case?

'Just after I passed my driving test, I was stopped at a traffic light when …'

'Yeah, well, I was travelling down to Chile on a student exchange thing and this girl sat next to me …'

'I was sitting on my own, waiting for a friend …'

Now listen to Track 74. Were you correct?

2 In the stories on Track 74, here is what the people actually said. Listen to Track 74 again and put the number of the story (1–3) in the brackets.

a Can I buy you a drink? [ ]
b Could you turn your stereo down? [ ]
c Do you want to meet up? [ ]
d Go and sit somewhere else. [ ]
e I work at the local hospital. [ ]
f I'd like that very much. [ ]
g I'm a journalist. [ ]
h I'm George Smith but people call me Tiny. [ ]
i I'm writing a story about it. [ ]
j Why are you flying to Chile? [ ]
k Why do people call you that? [ ]
l You look so angry that I can't help it! [ ]

●●● Pronunciation: moving stress

3 Listen to Track 75. The woman is saying *He had a nice smile* … in four different ways. Match them with the following sentence endings.

a … but his conversation was very boring.
b … but his friend didn't.
c … but now he always looks miserable.
d … but it wasn't a fantastic one.

Which word did the speaker stress in each case?

4 Try saying the following sentence out loud. Put the stress on a different word each time. How does this change the meaning of the sentence?

Her father doesn't want her to marry Ben.

5 Practice Work in pairs. Describe how you met your partner or how a couple you know met each other.

Grammar: direct and indirect speech

6 How does Jim report his conversation with Rhiannon? Complete exercises *a* and *b*. Look at **14B** and **14C** in the Mini-grammar.

a Jim gets a phone call from Rhiannon. What does Jim tell his friend Steve about the conversation as it is happening?

Example: *She says she's seen me in the canteen.*

b Jim waited outside the theatre at seven, but Rhiannon didn't come. How does Jim tell the story to his sister later that evening?

Example: *She said she'd seen me in the canteen.*

7 Choose the most appropriate form of the verb in brackets.

a He said that they (meet) .... on holiday last year.

b He said that they (fall) .... in love almost at once.

c He said that he (never / be) .... in love before.

d She said that she (have to) .... go home in two days.

e She said that she (can / not) .... stay for another week.

f She said that she (will) .... see him in three weeks.

g He said that he (have / not) .... seen her since that day.

h He said that he still (miss) .... her.

Check your answers by looking at 14C in the Mini-grammar.

What were the speaker's actual words in each case?

Example: *We met on holiday last year.*

8 Look at **14D** in the Mini-grammar. Report the following conversation.

Example: *He asked her if the seat was free.*

STEFANO: Is this seat free?
CRISTINA: Why are you asking?
STEFANO: What's your name?
CRISTINA: Why do you want to know?
STEFANO: Why do you ask so many questions?
CRISTINA: Are you going to buy me a coffee?
STEFANO: Do you want a coffee?
CRISTINA: What do you think?
STEFANO: I just don't know!

9 Speaking **Think of three things people have asked you or that they have told you to do recently. Tell the class.**

Examples: *My friend asked me if I had remembered to bring Anna's telephone number – and of course I'd forgotten.*
My flatmate told me not to forget to leave a note for the milkman.

Vocabulary: friends and enemies

10 Match the words in the box with the people in the pictures.

accomplice   acquaintance   ally   colleague   companion
comrade   enemy   friend   partner (x2)

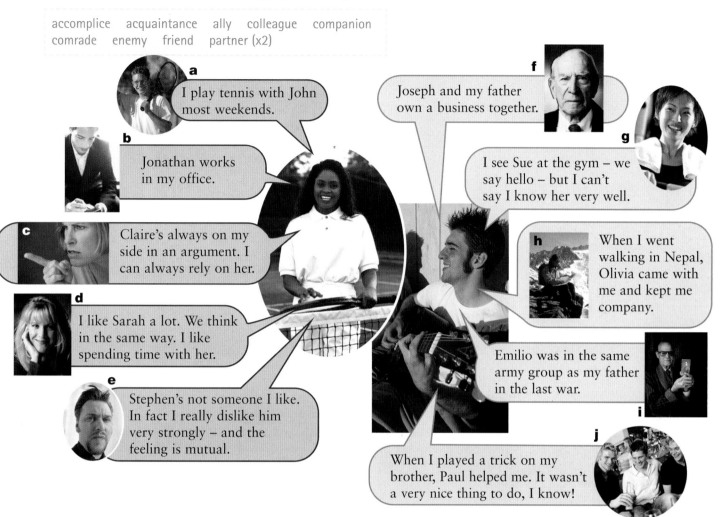

a I play tennis with John most weekends.

b Jonathan works in my office.

c Claire's always on my side in an argument. I can always rely on her.

d I like Sarah a lot. We think in the same way. I like spending time with her.

e Stephen's not someone I like. In fact I really dislike him very strongly – and the feeling is mutual.

f Joseph and my father own a business together.

g I see Sue at the gym – we say hello – but I can't say I know her very well.

h When I went walking in Nepal, Olivia came with me and kept me company.

i Emilio was in the same army group as my father in the last war.

j When I played a trick on my brother, Paul helped me. It wasn't a very nice thing to do, I know!

Using a dictionary: getting as much information as possible

11 Look at the entries for *adore*, *crazy* and *fond* and answer the questions.

   a Does *adore* take an object?
   b What can't you do when you use the verb *adore*?
   c When is *adore* rather informal?
   d What is the difference between the American and the British pronunciation of *fond*?
   e How common is the word *crazy* in English?
   f What is the superlative adjective form of *crazy*?
   g How many meanings are given for *crazy*? Which is the most common, do you think?
   h Which word or expression suggests that you have known someone for a long time?
   i Which word or expression has the strongest meaning, do you think?

12 Use each word or expression once to describe either a member of your family or something you like very much.

a·dore /əˈdɔː $ əˈdɔːr/ v [T not in progressive] **1** to love someone very much and feel very proud of them: *Betty adores her grandchildren.* **2** *informal* to like something very much: *I simply adore chocolate.*

cra·zy¹ [S3] [W3] /ˈkreɪzi/ *adj comparative* **crazier**, *superlative* **craziest**
1 **STRANGE** very strange or not sensible; ☰ **mad**: *The neighbours must think we're crazy.* | *It's an absolutely crazy idea.* | *I know this idea sounds crazy, but it may be worth a try.* | **crazy to do sth** *It'd be crazy to go out in this rain.* | *I must have been crazy to agree to this.* | *He often works 12 hours a day – it's crazy.*
2 **crazy about sb/sth** liking someone very much, or very interested in something: *He's crazy about her.* | *Dan's crazy about football.*
3 **ANGRY** angry or annoyed: *Turn that music down. It's driving me crazy* (=really annoying me)! | *Dad will go crazy when he hears about this.*
4 like crazy very much or very quickly: *We're going to have to work like crazy to get this finished on time.*
5 go crazy to do something too much, in a way that is not usual or sensible, especially because you are excited: *Don't go crazy and spend it all at once.*
6 **MENTALLY ILL** mentally ill; ☰ **mad**: *I feel so alone, sometimes I wonder if I'm going crazy.* —**crazily** *adv* —**craziness** *n* [U]

fond /fɒnd $ fɑːnd/ *adj* **1** be fond of sb to like someone very much, especially when you have known them for a long time and almost feel love for them: *Joe's quite fond of her, isn't he?* | *Over the years we've grown very fond of each other.* **2** be fond of (doing) sth to like something, especially something you have liked for a long time: *I'm not overly fond of cooking.* | *I'd grown fond of the place and it was difficult to leave.* **3** be fond of doing sth to do something often, especially something that annoys other people: *My grandfather was very fond of handing out advice to all my friends.* **4** [only before noun] a fond look, smile, action etc shows you like someone very much; ☰ **affectionate**: *He gave her a fond look.* | *As we parted we said a fond farewell.* **5** have fond memories of sth/sb to remember someone or something with great pleasure: *Marie still had fond memories of their time together.* **6** a fond hope/belief a belief or hope that something will happen, which seems silly because it is very unlikely to happen: *in the fond hope/belief that They sent him to another school in the fond hope that his behaviour would improve.* —**fondness** *n* [U]: *a fondness for expensive clothes* → FONDLY

13 Look at the following words. How can you say the opposite of each word or phrase? (Sometimes just using *not* will be enough.)

a admire g get along (fine / well)
b adore   (with)
c be close to h like
d be crazy about i love
e be fond of j respect
f be in love with k think a lot of

Where would you put your words (positive and negative) in the following diagram?

someone you know well

feeling very negative about someone ←——→ feeling very positive about someone

someone you don't know well

Compare your diagram with a partner's. Are your diagrams the same?

14 Write names of people in your own life for six of the following on a piece of paper – but don't say which they are.

> an accomplice   an acquaintance   an ally
> a colleague   a companion   a comrade
> an enemy   a friend   a partner

15 Show your list to a partner. They must find out (a) who the people are, and (b) what you think of them.

Example: STUDENT A: Who's Ali?

STUDENT B: He's my friend.

STUDENT A: How do you get on with him?

STUDENT B: I like him a lot. I admire him you see. We get along fine.

Speaking: a sad story (story reconstruction)

16 Work in groups. Put the pictures in order to tell a story.

17 Practice Tell your story to another group and listen to their story. Are the stories the same or different?

18 Turn to Activity Bank 7 on page 153 and read the story. How different is it from the stories you have heard?

Functional language: inviting someone

19 Before you listen to Track 76, put the following conversation in the correct order.

[**1**] Hi Carol.
[ ] Ainsley, what are you talking about?
[ ] Hello Ainsley.
[ ] Fantastic!
[ ] Is it? Well yes, I suppose it is.
[ ] It's a nice day.
[ ] Look, I was wondering, well that is, I had this idea and I thought perhaps, but perhaps not, I don't know.
[ ] Come to the cinema. With me.
[ ] You know what? That would be great.
[ ] That would be great.
[ ] Oh, well all right ... what did you say?
[ ] Would you like to come to the cinema tonight?
[ ] Would I like to what?

Now listen to Track 76. Were you correct?

20 Look at the following ways of inviting people out and say whether they are *Type 1* or *Type 2*.

> **Type 1:** quite formal (the speaker is nervous about asking the other person out)
> **Type 2:** quite casual (the speaker is more confident about asking the other person out)

a Are you on for the cinema?
b Do you fancy coming to the cinema?
c Do you want to go to the cinema?
d How about coming to the cinema?
e I was wondering if you would like to come to the cinema.
f There's a good movie on at the cinema – do you want to come?
g What about the cinema?
h Would you be interested in coming to the cinema?
i Would you like to come to the cinema?

21 Look at the following ways of responding to invitations and put them into the correct column.

yes   perhaps   no

a Could I let you know?
b Great! / Fantastic!
c I can't, I'm afraid.
d Not really, thanks all the same.
e I will if I can.
f It's very kind of you to invite me but I'm not sure if I can / don't think I can.
g Not sure if I can, actually.
h That sounds very nice.
i That's very kind of you.
j That's very kind of you but I'm afraid ...
k Yes, I'd love to.
l Yes, that would be marvellous.

22 Work in pairs. Make up a dialogue for one of the following situations using language from Activities 20 and 21.

a A young man finally finds the courage to ask a colleague to go for a coffee. The colleague quite likes him, but is not sure whether to agree to the invitation.
b A female student asks her male friend to go out. They go out together quite often.
c A woman asks a neighbour out. Unfortunately the neighbour doesn't want to go, but doesn't want to offend her.
d Two people meet at a party. One confidently asks the other out.

Act out your conversations for the class. They have to guess which situation it is.

Reading: Rachel

23 Read the text. It comes from a book called *Trumpet Voluntary*.
Do you think the book is:

a ... an instruction book for trumpet players?
b ... a story of romantic love?
c ... a study of one of the most famous pieces of 17th-century music?

I liked Rachel. She was quiet and gentle. She had light brown hair, and pretty brown eyes set in a round, pleasant face. When she smiled she looked like a happy child and you knew you could trust her. She was very easy to talk to.

That night we sat and talked about what we hoped for in the future. I told her I wanted to make enough money as a musician to have a nice house, travel a bit, that kind of thing. She told me that her dreams were much the same. She wanted children one day, she said, but for that she'd need to find the right man.

'Well it's no good looking at me,' I said, as a joke.

'I know that, you fool,' she said, laughing at me. 'You can't see anybody anyway. Not while Malgosia is in the way.' I blushed.

'Maybe,' I replied. I didn't like talking about it.

'Can I say something?' Rachel asked, nervously.

'It depends what it is,' I replied. Around us people were talking and laughing as the night got darker. I saw the lights of a party boat travelling along the river in front of us.

'It's just that, well, I know Malgosia is beautiful. I mean really beautiful. I wish I was beautiful like that. And I do like her. But she's crazy about Tibor, and anyone who's crazy about Tibor, well ... .' She stopped and looked at me, wondering how I would react.

'Well what?' I answered. I understood what she was saying, I think, but I didn't like anyone criticising Malgosia.

'Oh, now you're cross with me,' Rachel worried. 'Sorry. Sorry. But it's just a pity to see you and her. She's not right for you. You're wasting your time, wasting your life on her and you're not getting anything back. It doesn't look good. That's what I think.'

'Well,' I snapped back, without thinking, 'I don't care what you think, OK? Me and Malgosia, well, we're ... .' I wanted a word that meant more than 'friend' but I couldn't think of the right one. '... We're special, all right? So it's none of your business. Just keep out of my affairs, OK?'

Rachel had gone red and I had gone too far. My only excuse is that I was very confused then, and still very young. But I suppose, if I am honest, that wasn't it. It was because Rachel had said something that I didn't want to hear because it was the truth. Now I think that if only I had listened to her then, if only I had understood what she was trying to tell me, I might not have made the decisions that I did and my life might have turned out very differently.

24 Find words or phrases in the text, in Activity 23, with the following meanings. The first letter is given for each.

   a   a stupid person (f)
   b   to go red from embarrassment (b)
   c   to be really in love with someone (c, a)
   d   to say or do something because of what someone
        else has said or done (r)
   e   saying bad things about someone (c)
   f   angry (c)
   g   to say something suddenly because you are angry (s)

25 Read the text again. What do you know about these people?

   a   the narrator
   b   Rachel
   c   Tibor
   d   Malgosia

26 Without looking back at the text, rewrite these sentences with the correct punctuation.

   a   can I say something Rachel asked nervously
   b   I know that you fool she said laughing at me
   c   but she's crazy about Tibor and anyone who's crazy about Tibor well
   d   well what I answered
   e   well I snapped back without thinking I don't care what you think
        OK me and Malgosia well we're

27 Answer the following questions.

   a   When we close inverted commas, do we usually put punctuation
        marks (commas, question marks, etc.) before or after the inverted commas?
   b   How can we show that a speaker stops talking in the middle of a sentence?
   c   When we put a phrase like *he / she said* in between two parts of
        the same direct speech, what punctuation do we use?

Language in chunks

28 Complete these phrases from the text and explain what they mean.
   a   She was very easy ....
   b   She's not right ....
   c   You're wasting ....
   d   I don't care what ....
   e   ... it's none of ....
   f   Just keep out of ....
   g   I had gone ....

29 Which two phrases are used in an aggressive way?

30 Choose two of the phrases above and use them in sentences of your own.

31 The narrator says, 'If only I had listened to her then, ... my life might have turned out very differently.' What do you think he means? What do you think happened to him? Compare your answers with other pairs'.

Writing: 'small ads'

32 Look at the newspaper advertisements on the right (often called 'small ads'). Which one is looking for:

a ... someone to talk on the telephone all day?   [   ]
b ... a wife / girlfriend?   [   ]
c ... someone to work with cars?   [   ]
d ... a husband / boyfriend?   [   ]
e ... someone to work with food?   [   ]

33 Match the words in the box with their meanings (a–i).

> applicant   hygiene   good with people   mechanic
> negotiable   rate of pay   salary   the outdoor life   WLTM

a friendly and polite
b keeping things clean
c walking, cycling, etc.
d something that can be changed or agreed through discussion
e someone who asks someone for a job
f someone who fixes cars
g the money that is paid every month
h would like to meet
i the amount of money offered for a job

34 Complete the following sentences using words from the advertisements.

a .... Mary on 01229 ...
b .... negotiable.
c 50-something man .... happy, artistic woman.
d Cook .... for new restaurant.
e Experience .... but not essential.
f The successful .... will earn a lot of money.
g The applicant must .... people.

35 Advertisers pay for every word they use. They usually try to make their advertisements as cheap as possible. How do they do this? Give as many examples as you can from the advertisements.

36 Using words and phrases from the advertisements in Activities 33 and 34, write your own advertisement for one of the following:

a a cook for a restaurant
b a cleaner for a supermarket
c someone you would like to meet
d a receptionist for a garage

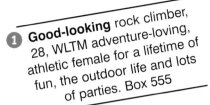

1 **Good-looking** rock climber, 28, WLTM adventure-loving, athletic female for a lifetime of fun, the outdoor life and lots of parties. Box 555

2 **Duty manager.** Salary £260 per week. Experienced person needed for busy self-service restaurant in Gratten Centre. Applicant must be good with people and be responsible for good hygiene standards. 5-day week, daytime only. Call Steve for interview (01̶5̶2̶2̶

3 Harland Motors requires full-time qualified mechanic. Start immediately. Must be reliable and self-motivated. Good rate of pay for the right applicant. Tel: Sam or Adi on 01533

4 **Female teacher**, 40-something, loves classical music, theatre, art, seeks honest, gentle, sensitive, capable and amusing man for marriage. Box 329

5 **TELESALES** person required for fast-growing company. Experience preferred. Salary, hours negotiable. Call Ruth on 01̶2̶8̶3̶

Review: grammar and functional language

37 Report the following conversation to a friend.

A: Hello! How are you?
YOU: I'm fine.
A: Are you doing anything this evening?
YOU: No, I don't think so.
A: Would you like to come to a film with me?
YOU: That depends on the film.
A: It's a very old film called *Love Story*. It's on at the local Arts Cinema.
YOU: With a title like that, I can't refuse!
A: So I'll see you at about eight o'clock?
YOU: Sure. I'm looking forward to it.

38 Complete the story with one word for each gap.

Noreen didn't like her (**a**) .... job but her colleagues seemed (**b**) .... , and when she looked (**c**) .... the office she thought she might make some friends there.

When she had (**d**) .... university three months ago, Noreen had wondered what (**e**) .... do. She had told her mother that she (**f**) .... to travel around the world but her (**g**) .... had said that this was not a good idea. Instead she had (**h**) .... Noreen to get a job. 'We're not made of money,' she had (**i**) .... , 'it's time you paid your own way.'

When a (**j**) .... asked Noreen if she would like to join a (**k**) .... of the people from the office at a restaurant one evening she was very (**l**) .... She told them she'd love to go.

It was a great evening. (**m**) .... seemed very friendly, and Noreen soon found that she was (**n**) .... along fine with the group. When she arrived home (**o**) .... old her mother she had had a fantastic evening. Her mother said she was (**p**) .... pleased and hoped that this was the end of Noreen's plans to (**q**) .... around the world. 'Well not really, Mum,' her (**r**) .... told her, 'a group is going to leave next month and they're travelling to five different countries. They've (**s**) .... me to go with them, and I've said yes!'

Write the conversations (including the direct speech extracts here) between:

a ... Noreen and her mother.
b ... Noreen and her colleagues.

39 Speaking People meet new friends in all kinds of places – on beaches, on a football pitch, in a restaurant. Where and how have you met your best friends? Ask others in the class.

Review: vocabulary

Word List

accomplice acquaintance admire adore ally applicant blush colleague companion comrade criticise cross enemy fool friend hygiene like love mechanic negotiable partner rate of pay react respect salary snap the outdoor life	

Word Plus

good with people	to be not right for
keep out of (my) affairs	someone / something
none of your business	to get along (fine / well)
to be close to	(with)
to be crazy about	to not care
to be easy to please	to think a lot of
to be fond of	to waste someone's time
to be in love with	

40 If you had to throw away four words from the Word List, which ones would you choose and why?

Example: *I'd throw away 'enemy' because I want to be friends with everyone.*

● ● ● Pronunciation

41 a Which words from the Word List do you find difficult to pronounce? Which sounds in those words do you think cause the problem?

b Write a sentence using at least one word from the Word List. Say the sentence, stressing a different word each time. How does changing the stress affect the meaning?

Example: *His wife is cross.* (But his sister is happy!)

42 Writing Using phrases from Word Plus, write sentences starting with *he*, *she* and *they*.

Example: *He's crazy about her but she doesn't care.*

Arrange your lines so they make a poem. Try changing the order of the lines. Which poem is best?

And, in the end ...

You have finished *Just Right*. How do you feel you have progressed? Write a personal assessment of your studies. Mention:

- ... things in the book you really liked.
- ... things you didn't like very much.
- ... areas where you think you have made progress.
- ... areas where you haven't made so much progress.
- ... how easy / difficult you find English.
- ... how English will be useful for you in the future.
- ... your plans for learning English in the future.

Activity Bank

1 [Unit 1]

Questionnaire key

Find out what your answers mean:

If you answered mostly a: you are often assertive, decisive, strong, and sincere. You are a good leader and the perfect person to follow in an emergency.

If you answered mostly b: you are often considerate, friendly, patient and honest. People trust you and they are right to do so.

If you answered mostly c: you are often emotional, kind, romantic and sympathetic. People turn to you when they have problems. You like to be with others and they like to be with you.

If you chose different letters each time you must have all of these characteristics.

2 [Unit 1]

Who did you meet at the party? Copy and complete the first two columns in the following table.

Role-playing name	Role-playing occupation (what you / they are doing)	

When the activity is over, write the real name of the student who played the role in the third column.

3 [Unit 1]

April Considine has just won the UK 'Young woman of the year' engineering award. After school she went to train as an apprentice with a company called Marshall's Aerospace in Cambridge, UK. She now works there as a design engineer. She is one of only six women in the company, where there are two hundred and fifty employees.

At Marshall's Aerospace customers often bring their aeroplanes to be changed in some way. Perhaps they want a new door, or new seats inside the plane. They might want to add something to the wing or have a new video system. It is April's job – along with her colleagues – to design the necessary modifications.

4 [Unit 4]

You are a travel agent. Write down information about the following holidays that you offer.

Package holiday:

Sightseeing holiday:

Cruise:

Activity holiday:

For each holiday decide on the following:

- Where it is
- Type of accommodation
- Description of area / sights to be seen
- Things to do
- Price

5 [Unit 9]

You are:

a ... angry.
b ... bored.
c ... enthusiastic.
d ... friendly.
e ... happy.
f ... interested.
g ... nervous.

h ... not telling the truth.
i ... relaxed.
j ... surprised.
k ... confident.
l ... impatient.
m ... sincere.

6 [Unit 11]

Types of book:	historical novel comic novel biography autobiography	romance detective story science fiction novel
Types of play:	musical opera play tragedy	comedy detective story thriller
Types of film:	action film animated film horror film war film	western romantic comedy thriller

7 [Unit 14]

A sad story

One day Michael saw Catherine sitting alone in a café. He thought she was beautiful. So he went over to her and started talking to her.
He rang her the next day and asked her out. Pretty soon they were boyfriend and girlfriend. But one day Catherine was walking in a park when she saw Michael with another girl. She was very angry and asked him what he was doing. The other girl soon became angry as well and they both told him to go and jump in the lake!

Now Michael just sits on his own every evening watching the sun go down and feeling miserable.

8 [Unit 2]

STUDENT A

Study the pictures and answer the questions about them.

1 What is the waiter waiting for?
2 How does Pete (the man sitting down) feel?
3 What is he remembering?

4 How many people are doing the washing-up?
5 Who else can you see in the picture?
6 How do the people (who are not doing the washing-up) feel, do you think?

Now turn back to Activity 30 on page 22.

9 [Unit 4]

GROUP A

SOME REASONS WHY TOURISM IS A BAD THING

According to many scientists, 15% of all greenhouse gases will come from aeroplanes by 2050.

The more aeroplanes there are in the sky, the more dangerous flying gets.

Tourism has a bad impact on places:

- Water is diverted from agricultural and / or poor areas.
- It generates a lot of rubbish.
- It destroys countryside that is built on.
- It destroys countryside that is walked on.
- It pushes wildlife away.
- It destroys traditional customs and ways of life.

10 [Unit 7]

STUDENT A

You're going to have a party at your house on Saturday night. Try and persuade the others to come.

11 [Unit 10]

Look at the picture of rock star Kate Springer's birthday party. Find out the missing names and information by asking Student B. Answer Student B's questions too.

Example: STUDENT B: *Who's Charlie Johnson?*

STUDENT A: *He's the journalist who wrote about Kate two years ago.*

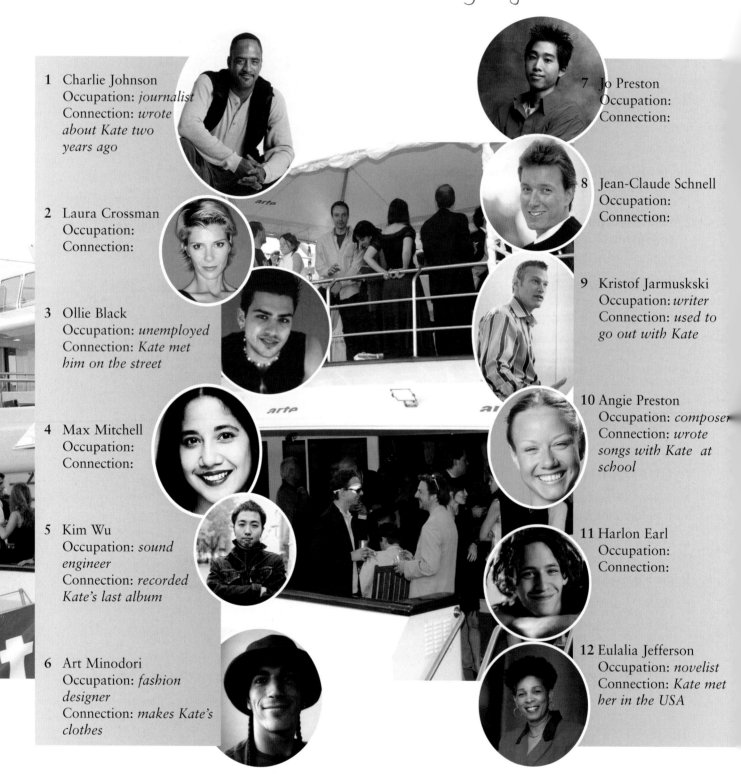

1 Charlie Johnson
Occupation: *journalist*
Connection: *wrote about Kate two years ago*

2 Laura Crossman
Occupation:
Connection:

3 Ollie Black
Occupation: *unemployed*
Connection: *Kate met him on the street*

4 Max Mitchell
Occupation:
Connection:

5 Kim Wu
Occupation: *sound engineer*
Connection: *recorded Kate's last album*

6 Art Minodori
Occupation: *fashion designer*
Connection: *makes Kate's clothes*

7 Jo Preston
Occupation:
Connection:

8 Jean-Claude Schnell
Occupation:
Connection:

9 Kristof Jarmuskski
Occupation: *writer*
Connection: *used to go out with Kate*

10 Angie Preston
Occupation: *composer*
Connection: *wrote songs with Kate at school*

11 Harlon Earl
Occupation:
Connection:

12 Eulalia Jefferson
Occupation: *novelist*
Connection: *Kate met her in the USA*

Have you got a photograph of a group of people you know? If you have, show it to your partner and tell them who the people are and what connection they have to you.

12 [Unit 11]

STUDENT A

Describe this picture to your partner so that they can draw it. You must not show your picture to your partner until they have finished their drawing.

13 [Unit 13]

STUDENT A

Read the text and make sure you understand the answers to the following questions.

a Why was there a queue of people in the street?
b What happened at four o'clock?
c How many people died?
d When exactly did they die?
e Who were they?
f Who is or was Vedran Smailovic?

In the early 1990s, there was a terrible war in Yugoslavia. Many people died, both soldiers and civilians. The city of Sarajevo was for many months one of the most dangerous places in the world. It was constantly under attack and its civilian inhabitants had to live with no electricity and little water. Only a few shops stayed open to sell food.

On May 27, 1992, one of the shops, a bakery, opened in the afternoon and a long line of men, women and children queued to buy fresh bread. But it was not to be. At four o'clock a mortar shell exploded in the street and twenty-two innocent people were killed.

A man called Vedran Smailovic lived near the scene of this terrible tragedy. He was 35 at the time, and when he heard the news he decided to do something about it.

Find answers to the following questions by asking Students B and C. Don't show them your text.

a What was Vedran Smailovic's job before the war?
b What extraordinary thing did Vedran Smailovic do when he heard the news?
c Who played David Wilde's piece for solo cello?
d Who was in the audience when the piece was first performed?

14 [UNIT 2]

Study the pictures and answer the questions about them.

1 Who are Pete and Tabitha talking to?
2 What is Pete trying to explain?

3 Where is Pete?
4 Why has he gone there?
5 What can he see inside the house?

Now turn back to Activity 30 on page 22.

15 [Unit 4]

GROUP B

SOME REASONS WHY TOURISM IS A GOOD THING

Tourism is fun.

Tourism benefits local economies.

Tourism is the world's largest industry.

Tourism provides employment to many who otherwise would have no jobs.

Tourism helps peoples of the world to understand each other.

If you restrict tourism, only the rich will be able to travel.

Everyone needs a chance to unwind. Tourism provides this.

16 [Unit 7]

STUDENT B

You're going to go for a meal at a local restaurant on Saturday night.
Try to persuade the others to come.

STUDENT B

Look at the picture of rock star Kate Springer's birthday party. Find out the missing names and information by asking Student A. Answer Student A's questions too.

Example: STUDENT B: *Who's Charlie Johnson?*

STUDENT A: *He's the journalist who wrote about Kate two years ago.*

1 Charlie Johnson
  Occupation:
  Connection:

2 Laura Crossman
  Occupation: *photographer*
  Connection: *took photos for Kate's first album*

3 Ollie Black
  Occupation:
  Connection:

4 Max Mitchell
  Occupation: *tennis player*
  Connection: *Kate watched her play yesterday*

5 Kim Wu
  Occupation:
  Connection:

6 Art Minodori
  Occupation:
  Connection:

7 Jo Preston
  Occupation: *hairdresser*
  Connection: *he lived next door to Kate after she left school*

8 Jean-Claude Schnell
  Occupation: *chauffeur*
  Connection: *drives Kate to all her concerts*

9 Kristof Jarmuskski
  Occupation:
  Connection:

10 Angie Preston
   Occupation:
   Connection:

11 Harlon Earl
   Occupation: *guitarist*
   Connection: *Kate wants to develop a friendship with him*

12 Eulalia Jefferson
   Occupation:
   Connection:

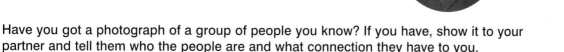

Have you got a photograph of a group of people you know? If you have, show it to your partner and tell them who the people are and what connection they have to you.

18 [Unit 7]

STUDENT C

You're going to go dancing at a club on Saturday night. Try to persuade the others to come.

19 [Unit 11]

STUDENT B

Describe this picture to your partner so that they can draw it. You must not show your picture to your partner until they have finished their drawing.

20 [Unit 13]

STUDENT B

Read the text and make sure you understand the answers to the following questions.

a What was Vedran Smailovic's job before the war?
b What did Vedran Smailovic do when he heard the news?
c What piece of music did he play?
d Why did he play his cello?
e Was he ever hurt?

Before the war, Vedran Smailovic had been a cellist with the Sarajevo Opera. When he heard about an explosion that had killed men, women and children in a bread queue in Sarajevo, he decided to do something about it. And so he did what he did best. He played his cello.

For the next twenty-two days at exactly four o'clock in the afternoon he put on his concert clothes, took his cello and a plastic chair into the empty streets and played a piece of music by the composer Albinoni – his Adagio in G minor, one of the saddest pieces of music ever. Around him there was fighting and death. Shells fell and bullets flew while he played, but he was never hurt. With the world collapsing around him he played for compassion and peace, to ease the pain of loss and to preserve the dignity of the human race.

Find the answers to the following questions by asking Students A and C. Don't show your text to them.

a Why did Vedran Smailovic play for twenty-two days?
b Why did he play at four o'clock in the afternoon?
c Who is David Wilde and what did he do?
d What is David Wilde's connection to a concert in Manchester?

21 [Unit 7]

You're going to go to see a film at the local cinema on Saturday night. Try to persuade the others to come.

22 [Unit 13]

STUDENT C

Read the text and make sure you understand the answers to the following questions.

a Who is David Wilde?
b What did he read about?
c What did he do then?
d Where was the first UK performance of his new music?
e Who played it?
f Who was in the audience?

David Wilde, an English composer, read a story in his newspaper which moved him deeply. It was about a man called Vedran Smailovic, who played his cello in the street in the middle of a war to honour the dead. His courage was extraordinary because he sat in the street and played while shells and bullets flew around him.

David Wilde was so inspired by the story that he wrote a special piece for solo cello which he called *The Cellist of Sarajevo*. It was performed by the cellist YoYo Ma at the Manchester Cello Festival in April 1994. Incredibly, Vedran Smailovic had survived the war and was in the audience that night to hear it. When YoYo Ma finished playing, the two men embraced in front of a cheering audience.

Find the answers to the following questions by asking Students A and B. Don't show your text to them.

a Exactly what happened in Sarajevo on May 27, 1992?
b What was Vedran Smailovic's job before the war?
c Why did Vedran Smailovic play his cello? What piece of music did he play?

23 [Unit 7]

STUDENT E

You're not sure what you would like to do. Listen to the others and then agree to do something with one of them.